Cooking with
Yogurt

Hamlyn Cookshelf Series

Cooking with Yogurt

Beth Cockburn-Smith

Hamlyn
London · New York · Sydney · Toronto

To Mattie
with love and thanks

The following titles are also available in this series:

The Food Processor Cookbook · Mighty Mince Cookbook
Potato Cookery · Sweets and Candies

The author and publisher would like to thank the following
for their help in sponsoring photographs for this book:
Birds Eye Foods Limited page 34
British Poultry Meat Association page 52
New Zealand Lamb Information Bureau page 51
The Pasta Information Centre page 85

The publisher would also like to thank the
Milk Marketing board for their help and advice.

Front cover photograph by James Jackson
Photography by Paul Williams
Line illustrations Joanna Troughton

First published in 1980 by The Hamlyn Publishing Group Limited
London · New York · Sydney · Toronto
Astronaut House, Feltham, Middlesex, England

This edition published in 1984
© Copyright The Hamlyn Publishing Group Limited 1980, 1984

ISBN 0 600 32426 5

Phototypeset in Great Britain
by Servis Filmsetting Limited, Manchester

Printed in Yugoslavia

Contents

Useful Facts and Figures

Notes on metrication
In this book quantities are given in metric, Imperial and American measures. Exact conversion from Imperial to metric measures does not usually give very convenient working quantities and so the metric measures have been rounded off into units of 25 grams. The table below shows the recommended equivalents.

guide, 1 kg (1000 g) equals 2.2 lb or about 2 lb 3 oz. This method of all cases, although in certain pastry and cake recipes a more accurate conversion is necessary to produce a balanced recipe.

Liquid measures The millilitre has been used in this book and the following table gives a few examples.

Ounces	Approx g to nearest whole figure	Recommended conversion to nearest unit of 25
1	28	25
2	57	50
3	85	75
4	113	100
5	142	150
6	170	175
7	198	200
8	227	225
9	255	250
10	283	275
11	312	300
12	340	350
13	368	375
14	396	400
15	425	425
16 (1 lb)	454	450
17	482	475
18	510	500
19	539	550
20 ($1\frac{1}{4}$ lb)	567	575

Imperial	Approx ml to nearest whole figure	Recommended ml
$\frac{1}{4}$ pint	142	150ml
$\frac{1}{2}$ pint	283	300ml
$\frac{3}{4}$ pint	425	450ml
1 pint	567	600ml
$1\frac{1}{2}$ pints	851	900ml
$1\frac{3}{4}$ pints	992	1000ml (1 litre)

Spoon measures All spoon measures given in this book are level unless otherwise stated.
Can sizes At present, cans are marked with the exact (usually to the nearest whole number) metric equivalent of the Imperial weight of the contents, so we have followed this practice when giving can sizes.
Flour Unless specified, either plain or self-raising flour can be used in the recipes.
Yogurt Yogurt throughout refers to natural unsweetened yogurt. For ease and consistency we have given yogurt measures in fractions of a litre/pint/cup; the average individual pot of yogurt bought commercially holds approximately 150 ml/$\frac{1}{4}$ pint or 5 fl oz/$\frac{2}{3}$ cup.

Note When converting quantities over 20 oz first add the appropriate figures in the centre column, then adjust to the nearest unit of 25. As a general guide, 1 kg (1000g) equals 2.2 lb or

6

Oven temperatures
The table below gives recommended equivalents.

	°C	°F	Gas Mark
Very cool	110	225	$\frac{1}{4}$
	120	250	$\frac{1}{2}$
Cool	140	275	1
	150	300	2
Moderate	160	325	3
	180	350	4
Moderately hot	190	375	5
	200	400	6
Hot	220	425	7
	230	450	8
Very hot	240	475	9

Notes for American and Australian users
In America the 8-oz measuring cup is used. In Australia metric measures are now used in conjunction with the standard 250-ml measuring cup. The Imperial pint, used in Britain and Australia, is 20 fl oz, while the American pint is 16 fl oz. It is important to remember that the Australian tablespoon differs from both the British and American tablespoons, the table below gives a comparison. The British standard tablespoon, which has been used throughout this book, holds 17.7 ml, the American 14.2 ml, and the Australian 20 ml. A teaspoon holds approximately 5 ml in all three countries.

British	American	Australian
1 teaspoon	1 teaspoon	1 teaspoon
1 table-spoon	1 table-spoon	1 table-spoon
2 table-spoons	3 table-spoons	2 table-spoons
$3\frac{1}{2}$ table-spoons	4 table-spoons	3 table-spoons
4 table-spoons	5 table-spoons	$3\frac{1}{2}$ table-spoons

American terms
Although the recipes in this book give American measures and ingredients, the list below gives some equivalents or substitutes for terms and equipment which may be unfamiliar to American readers.

British/American
absorbent paper/paper towels
baking tray/baking sheet
cling film/saran wrap
cocktail stick/toothpick
double saucepan/double boiler
dough or mixture/batter
flan tin/pie pan
foil/aluminum foil
frying pan/skillet
greaseproof paper/wax paper
grill/broil(er)
hard-boil eggs/hard-cook eggs
liquidise/blend
loaf tin/loaf pan
mould/mold
muslin/cheesecloth
packet/package
polythene/plastic
pudding basin/ovenproof bowl
roasting tin/roasting pan
stoned/pitted
top and tail fruit/stem fruit
whisk eggs/beat eggs

Note: When making any of the recipes in this book, only follow one set of measures as they are not interchangeable.

Introduction

There is a new interest in food and drink in the Western World – no doubt about it. The subject of food, once banned from polite conversation at table, is now a fascinating topic, no longer confined to 'women's talk' either. The traditional roles of the man who went out to get food and the woman who stayed home to prepare it, are now both equally shared. And there is a new element of concern about the effect of what we eat on our health.

This concern has led to an awareness of the hazards of pre-packaged, so called convenience foods. Most people now avoid them and prefer natural wholefoods, recognising that these are almost always better, and less expensive too. Manufacturers of processed foods in England and America are now obliged to list the contents; and consequently, better late than never, a lot of horrific and highly toxic flavourings, preservatives and colourings have been withdrawn from the market.

Although not absolutely proven, it is now accepted commonsense thinking that men, in particular, will live longer if they reduce the intake of animal fats and increase the fibre content in their diets. Although women need not, in general, be so concerned about their cholesterol level or the danger of heart disease, they will certainly benefit by being slimmer, and by aiding the body in a natural way.

Yes, there has certainly been a revolution in the kitchen – the Bocuse and Guérard 'nouvelle cuisine' is no longer new, and has come to stay. A new enjoyment in the preparation of food, coupled with a determination to nourish not poison the body, has brought cooking to something between a hobby and an art form for most amateur enthusiasts.

This book on cooking with yogurt is a celebration of such new enthusiasm. Its aim is to inspire you to head straight for the kitchen!

Yogurt is a wonder food: high in vitamins, protein and calcium, low in calories. It is a versatile and invaluable food, easily digested by young and old, marvellous on its own or as a basic ingredient in countless recipes. Unless preaching to the converted, it is difficult to exaggerate the good qualities of yogurt – and what's more it *Tastes* good too!

Beth Cockburn-Smith

All About Yogurt

Yogurt is one of the oldest foods in the world; the very first 'convenience food', invaluable for its exceptional nourishment and its ability to last longer than fresh milk. It has only quite recently become known in the West but has already gained enormous popularity. Yogurt has come a long way from the skin pouches of the Asian nomads who accidentally discovered it. The bags in which they carried their milk were made from the lining of sheep's stomachs – and here were the beneficial bacteria that fermented the milk in the warmth of the sun. Soon, in those very early days, women learned to boil milk and inoculate it with a small amount of yogurt to make a fresh bowl, and it is still made in the same way by women in their kitchens today.

A kind of magic hangs about the subject still, in spite of all the scientific research and up to date knowledge. There are many references from ancient cultures in Central Asia, the Near and Middle East, and the Balkan countries of South Eastern Europe. Students of the bible believe the Promised Land to have flowed with 'laban' (the word still used for yogurt) and honey, rather than milk and honey. There is a reference in Genesis to Abraham offering yogurt to the three men who brought him the news of Isaac's birth, and tradition credits his longevity and fertility to the eating of yogurt. There is a lovely story, now famous, about François I of France who was suffering from an apparently incurable stomach complaint. He heard of a remarkable cure effected by a Turkish doctor and sent for him in desperation. The healer arrived on foot with his herd of goats, gave the King yogurt to eat and cured him completely. But he then went on his way, refusing to give up the secret of his 'medicine'. A Nineteenth Century director of the Pasteur Institute, Ilya Mechnikov, while studying senility and the causes of ageing in humans, was impressed by the fabulously fit old people in Bulgaria who continued to work in the fields and father and bear children far beyond the normal expected age. Their diet included a considerable amount of yogurt and he eventually came to the conclusion that this was the secret of their good health. His studies led to isolating the two basic bacteria, Streptococcus thermophilus and Lactobacillus bulgaricus. His theory was that these bacteria have a beneficial effect on the intestine, controlling harmful bacteria which normally stay there over long periods to poison the body and hasten the ageing process.

Recipes using yogurt come from all over the world: Bulgaria, famous for its fabulous gulyás and paprika dishes; Russia and Scandinavia; India, where yogurt is widely used in and with curries, as a marinade to flavour and tenderise meat, and to make a refreshing drink called ihassi; Greece, whose delicious yogurt is served with honey as a dessert and is also made into numerous dishes such as tzatziki; Persia, whence the Arabian appetiser on page 37 is one of our favourites; France, where they are bigger yogurt consumers than we in Britain, and use it so extensively in cooking to replace cream and soured cream.

Yogurt can be made at home by boiling milk, cooling the milk to about blood heat, adding a small amount of ready made yogurt to this and keeping it warm until it sets. It can also be made from a yogurt plant. This is not one of the myths like the spaghetti tree, and it doesn't live in a pot on the kitchen window sill either! Small white granular balls like to be kept in a bowl and fed milk. To make yogurt pour 600 ml/1 pint (U.S. $2\frac{1}{2}$ cups) of fresh milk on to the plant and leave, covered, in the warmth of the kitchen for about 24 hours. Strain the yogurt through a nylon sieve and chill it. Wash the yogurt plant thoroughly in cold water and squeeze dry. Feed it a little milk and store it in the refrigerator until you want to use it again. The plant grows and you may be lucky enough to be given some by a friend who has more than needed.

An ideal breakfast is yogurt, muesli and fruit; the rough-with-the-smooth combination is a perfect start to the day. Fresh flavoured, nourishing and easily digested, it is infinitely preferable to packaged breakfast cereals and fatty fried foods.

Yogurt can be used as a beauty treatment; model girls wash their faces in it, Audrey Hepburn uses yogurt as a face mask! Mix it with oatmeal, strawberries, honey or other natural ingredients as a tonic and pick-me-up for the skin.

Natural yogurt contains more of the B vitamins thiamine and riboflavine than milk, and more protein. Exceptionally rich in calcium, it also contains iron, phosphorus and potassium. Yogurt is of immense value to anyone on a cholesterol lowering diet as a substitute for cream and soured cream. The bacteria converts lactose (or sugar) in milk and because it is normally made from low fat skimmed milk, yogurt contains fewer calories than milk and is an ideal food for slimmers.

Deliciously creamy and slightly tart, yogurt certainly is a wonder food. Make full use of it, with fruit (both fresh and dried), honey, nuts, raw vegetables and on its own. Combine it with fish, eggs, meat, and poultry. Use it in vegetarian dishes, and to replace cream and soured cream so marvellously in dishes such as Boeuf Stroganoff and Vichyssoise. Be adventurous and imaginative with yogurt and you will reap its benefits in flavour, in beauty and in health.

Homemade Yogurt

Metric/Imperial	American
600 ml–1·15 litres/1–2 pints fresh milk	2½–5 cups fresh milk
150 ml/¼ pint natural yogurt (1 small carton)	⅔ cup plain yogurt

Bring the milk to a full boil so that it rises to the top of the pan and remains there for 1–2 minutes. Cool to 43°C/110°F, or so that your finger can stay in it comfortably for at least 10 seconds. Stir the yogurt thoroughly into the warm milk and cover with cling film. Put into a warm place (or a wide-mouthed thermos, scalded and heated) for about 5–10 hours, depending on the warmth, or transfer to an electric yogurt maker. Take out as soon as it has set. Stir the yogurt again, re-cover and chill in the refrigerator. This chilling halts the activity of the bacteria. Keep back 3 tablespoons (U.S. ¼ cup) for your next 'starter'.

Here are a few hints for a successful brew.

1 The 'starter' yogurt must be fresh, preferably not more than a day or two old, so buy from a supermarket with a fast turnover and examine the date mark. If you buy it from a small local shop, ask them the day of the week on which they take delivery of fresh yogurt, and buy and make your yogurt on that day.

2 Use clean utensils and equipment to inhibit activity from other bacteria.

3 The yogurt should be left undisturbed and away from vibrations while it is being made.

4 Natural yogurt will keep longer than yogurt to which fruit has been added. Natural yeasts in the fruit will cause the yogurt to become 'blown' or fizzy, so only add them on the day the yogurt is to be eaten.

5 If your yogurt turns acid it is probably because it was incubated for too long, or at too high a temperature, or possibly a slightly stale carton of yogurt was used in which the balance of bacteria had altered.

6 Thin 'sweet' yogurt is probably incubated at too low a temperature.

Dried lytholised milk ferments can be bought in sachets and make a useful standby as they will keep like this for several years in a cool place, and can be used as a starter instead of fresh yogurt. But a carton of yogurt is much less costly and produces equally good results.

Your yogurt will not be quite so uniformly smooth as commercial yogurt, because it has not been homogenised. It may also be thinner because commercial yogurt has 12–16% added milk solids. You can thicken yours with the addition of 1 tablespoon of skimmed milk powder to 600 ml/1 pint (U.S. $2\frac{1}{2}$ cups) milk. Add this at the start of yogurt making. Longlife U.H.T. milk and Longlife U.H.T. skimmed milk are very useful and easy for making yogurt, as they are already sterile, so simply warm to blood heat and add the starter yogurt. Treat as fresh milk from this point on.

All the recipes in this book are made using the basic natural yogurt, without sweetening or flavouring, but once you have made your basic yogurt, you can vary the flavour and texture in all sorts of ways; mix it with freshly chopped fruit, or a sweetened purée of cooked fruit, fresh or dried, add chopped nuts, raisins and sultanas, stir in honey or jam to sweeten, or simply soft brown sugar. For a savoury dish it is delicious mixed with just a few freshly chopped herbs from the garden, finely chopped olives or onions or even a little curry powder.

Making your own yogurt means that you always have plenty for yourself and your family. It is less expensive, and I am convinced that the flavour is better.

Yogurt Cheese aux Fines Herbes

Makes 100–175g/4–6 oz (U.S. $\frac{1}{2}$–$\frac{3}{4}$ cup)

Metric/Imperial	American
600 ml/1 pint yogurt	*$2\frac{1}{2}$ cups yogurt*
sea salt and freshly ground white pepper	*coarse salt and freshly ground white pepper*
2 tablespoons freshly chopped herbs (parsley, chervil and chives)	*3 tablespoons freshly chopped herbs (parsley, chervil and chives)*

Line a sieve or colander with muslin, empty the yogurt into it and place over a bowl. When it has drained for an hour or so, gather up the ends and tie them into a knot. Hang this from a hook over the bowl, or from the taps in the kitchen sink, to drain overnight. Keep the liquid to use in soup.

Stir in salt and pepper and shape the cheese into a flattish round. Sprinkle the herbs on to a board and press the cheese on to them, first one side and then the other. Sprinkle more herbs and then turn the cheese on them like a wheel, so that it is completely coated. Wrap in cling film and chill. Serve with butter curls and wholemeal or bran biscuits.

Note This can also be made without the fines herbes, when it is simply a plain yogurt cheese. If it is to accompany fruit, or to be used in sweet dishes, it should also of course be unseasoned.

Fromage Blanc

Makes about 225 g/8 oz (U.S. 1 cup)

This is an essential ingredient in the
cuisine minceur (or slenderness cooking)
of Monsieur Michel Guérard. His recipes
call for its use as a replacement for all sorts
of more fattening foods. It serves as a
liaison and thickening in sauces, and as a
basis for blanquettes and many chicken,
fish and veal recipes. It can also be served
with soft fruit and generally used to cut
down on the cholesterol and calories of
cream. The true fromage blanc is almost
unobtainable in this country, so here is my
version of how to make your own.

Metric/Imperial	American
100 g/4 oz yogurt cheese (see page 15) or cottage cheese	$\frac{1}{2}$ cup yogurt cheese (see page 15) or cottage cheese
6 tablespoons yogurt	$\frac{1}{2}$ cup yogurt
2 teaspoons lemon juice	2 teaspoons lemon juice

Liquidise the ingredients thoroughly in your blender or food
processor. Store in the refrigerator and use as necessary. Double the
quantities if you need more.

Breakfasts

Yogurt is the perfect breakfast food because it is light, fresh, nourishing and instant. Just eat it on its own for a good start to a rushed and busy day, or better still combine it with a dish of muesli and fruit.

Sunday brunch is a lovely way to entertain friends, and a large bowl of yogurt can provide the centre piece of the table. Surround it with satellite bowls of muesli, peeled and sliced oranges, stewed apricots, chopped apples, sliced bananas, grapes and strawberries, peaches, raspberries and loganberries in season. Provide smaller mounds of milled nuts, wheatgerm, brown sugar and raisins, and mix honey and apple juice in a jug to sweeten.

Place a basket of warm wholewheat rolls by a plate of smoked mackerel fillets, and accompany a hot dish of scrambled eggs with grilled bacon and mushrooms. Pile croissants under a napkin near butter curls, marmalade, cherry jam and a honey comb. Provide fresh orange juice, coffee, chilled champagne (for Buck's Fizz) and *all* the Sunday papers.

There are some more tempting breakfast suggestions in the following chapter.

Muesli

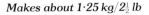

Makes about 1·25 kg/2½ lb

Here is the basic muesli recipe that we mix
with fruit and yogurt every morning for
breakfast. Store it in an airtight container.
Multiply by four if you eat it regularly and
are a big family.

Metric/Imperial	*American*
450 g/1 lb mixed grains (porridge oats, wheat flakes etc.)	1 lb mixed grains (porridge oats, wheat flakes etc.)
100 g/4 oz bran	2½ cups bran
100 g/4 oz wheatgerm	1 cup wheatgerm
2 tablespoons chopped walnuts	3 tablespoons chopped walnuts
2 tablespoons chopped hazelnuts	3 tablespoons chopped hazelnuts
2 tablespoons dried skimmed milk powder	3 tablespoons dried skimmed milk powder
100 g/4 oz dried vine fruits (raisins etc.)	¾ cup dried vine fruits (raisins etc.)
100 g/4 oz soft brown sugar	½ cup light brown sugar
100 g/4 oz ground almonds	1 cup ground almonds

Mix all the ingredients together. Add anything else to your own taste,
e.g. chopped dates, desiccated coconut. Serve with a bowl of yogurt,
and some fresh or stewed fruit.

Apple Muesli Yogurt

Serves 4

The help yourself muesli-yogurt-fruit breakfast can be varied infinitely. Here is a suggestion for a prepared mixture, and of course you will think of many others.

Metric/Imperial	American
2 tablespoons runny honey	3 tablespoons runny honey
2 tablespoons apple juice	3 tablespoons apple juice
2 red dessert apples, grated	2 red dessert apples, grated
juice of $\frac{1}{2}$ lemon	juice of $\frac{1}{2}$ lemon
600 ml/1 pint yogurt	$2\frac{1}{2}$ cups yogurt
175 g/6 oz muesli	$1\frac{1}{2}$ cups muesli

Mix the honey and apple juice and pour over the grated apples with the lemon juice. Combine this with the yogurt and muesli. It can be prepared the night before, or at breakfast time if you prefer it still to be crunchy.

American Pancakes

Makes about 8

Metric/Imperial	American
100 g/4 oz plain flour, sifted	1 cup all-purpose flour, sifted
$\frac{1}{2}$ teaspoon salt	$\frac{1}{2}$ teaspoon salt
2 teaspoons castor sugar (for sweet batters only)	2 teaspoons sugar (for sweet batters only)
4 eggs	4 eggs
300 ml/$\frac{1}{2}$ pint milk	$1\frac{1}{4}$ cups milk
50 g/2 oz butter, melted	$\frac{1}{4}$ cup melted butter

Combine the dry ingredients in a mixing bowl. Beat in the eggs and milk and finally the melted butter. Alternatively, mix the ingredients in a blender or food processor, adding the butter last.

Heat a small to medium-sized frying pan over a gentle to moderate heat. Rub the base of the pan with a piece of absorbent paper dipped in oil, and pour in just enough batter to coat the bottom; there should be a slight sizzling noise to tell you that the pan is hot enough. When tiny bubbles appear in the pancake, and the underneath is golden, toss the pancake in the air to turn and cook the other side.

The pancakes can be stacked and kept warm, or reheated over a pan of boiling water.

Savoury fillings Sautéed chicken livers with a few spoonfuls of yogurt, seasoned with freshly ground black pepper; crisp bacon pieces tossed with sautéed mushrooms and yogurt; red caviar with yogurt and dill weed; eggs scrambled with yogurt and grated Cheddar cheese.

Sweet fillings Sliced strawberries sprinkled with castor sugar, mixed with yogurt or cream; a sweetened purée of cooked dried apricots blended with yogurt; pancakes spread with honey, topped with banana slices in yogurt, rolled up, brushed with melted butter and flashed under the grill.

Louise's Yogurt with Brown Sugar

Serves 4

Metric/Imperial   **American**
900 ml/1½ pints yogurt   3¾ cups yogurt
4 tablespoons dark soft brown   ⅓ cup dark brown sugar
sugar

Make a nice thick batch of yogurt (add a spoonful of dried skimmed milk powder to the milk when making your yogurt). When set, leave to chill in the refrigerator in the bowl from which you will serve it.

Sprinkle the brown sugar on top, cover and leave overnight. By morning the yogurt will be bathed in a runny syrup which marbles the yogurt as it is served.

Note This can also be served as a delicious dessert as it is, or mixed with chopped fresh fruit, topped with a layer of soft brown sugar and caramelised under a hot grill to make a fruit brûlée.

All-Bran Fruit Loaf

Makes 1 loaf

Take the rough with the smooth and
combine the contrasting textures of bran
and yogurt to make a delicious sticky
bread.

Metric/Imperial	American
100 g/4 oz All-Bran	*2½ cups All-Bran*
100 g/4 oz soft brown sugar	*½ cup light brown sugar*
275 g/10 oz mixed dried fruit	*2 cups mixed dried fruit*
grated rind and juice of 1 orange	*grated rind and juice of 1 orange*
250 ml/8 fl oz yogurt	*1 cup yogurt*
100 g/4 oz self-raising 81% farmhouse flour	*1 cup whole wheat flour, mixed with 1 teaspoon baking . powder*

Put the All-Bran, sugar, dried fruit and orange rind into a bowl. Pour over the orange juice and yogurt (which should combine to make 300 ml/½ pint (U.S. 1¼ cups) liquid). Cover and leave to stand for 30 minutes. Stir in the flour and turn the mixture into a well greased 1-kg/2-lb loaf tin.

Bake the loaf in a moderate oven (180 C, 350 F, Gas Mark 4) for about 1¼ hours. Turn out of the tin and allow to cool on a wire tray. Cut into thin slices and spread with butter.

Banana Bread

Makes 2 loaves

Metric/Imperial	American
75 g/3 oz butter or polyunsaturated margarine	$\frac{1}{3}$ cup butter or polyunsaturated margarine
200 g/7 oz soft brown sugar	$\frac{3}{4}$ cup plus 2 tablespoons light brown sugar
275 g/10 oz self-raising 81% farmhouse flour	$2\frac{1}{2}$ cups whole wheat flour, mixed with $2\frac{1}{2}$ teaspoons baking powder
$\frac{1}{4}$ teaspoon salt	$\frac{1}{4}$ teaspoon salt
150 ml/$\frac{1}{4}$ pint yogurt	$\frac{2}{3}$ cup yogurt
4 bananas, peeled and mashed	4 bananas, peeled and mashed
grated rind of 1 lemon	grated rind of 1 lemon
2 eggs, lightly beaten	2 eggs, lightly beaten

Cream together the butter and sugar. Mix the flour with the salt. Combine the yogurt, bananas, lemon rind and eggs in a bowl. Beat this banana and yogurt mixture gradually into the butter and sugar, adding a spoonful of flour each time after the first addition. Fold in the remaining flour.

Turn into two greased and floured 0·5-kg/1-lb loaf tins and bake in a moderate oven (180°C, 350°F, Gas Mark 4) for $1\frac{1}{2}$ hours, or until a skewer inserted into the centre comes out clean.

Soups

Fresh soups offer such a variety of choice that they are right for almost any occasion. They can be served chilled or hot, creamy, crunchy or clear, thick or thin, elegant or hearty. Usually inexpensive, they are however a compliment to your guests as they always involve a little care and thought.

Yogurt is an invaluable piquant addition to many soups and can be used freely instead of cream or soured cream.

To prevent yogurt from curdling and separating in a hot soup, mix a teaspoon of cornflour with a little yogurt in a cup and add this first to the hot soup. Then stir in the rest of the yogurt and reheat but do not boil.

Allow the flavours to blend and intensify by letting the basic soup stand for 2 hours or more before reheating and adding the garnish.

Plan your soups around the fresh vegetables and ingredients of the season, when they are at their most tempting, and garnish with imagination but restraint.

Potage Crème Seychelles

Serves 4–6

Metric/Imperial	American
1·15 litres/2 pints good chicken stock	5 cups good chicken stock
1 small pineapple	1 small pineapple
50 g/2 oz butter	$\frac{1}{4}$ cup butter
2 tablespoons flour	3 tablespoons flour
1 teaspoon ground cumin	1 teaspoon ground cumin
150 ml/$\frac{1}{4}$ pint thick yogurt	$\frac{2}{3}$ cup thick yogurt
150 ml/$\frac{1}{4}$ pint single cream	$\frac{2}{3}$ cup light cream
salt and pepper	salt and pepper
1 tablespoon freshly chopped coriander leaves	1 tablespoon freshly chopped coriander leaves
1 tablespoon freshly chopped chives	1 tablespoon freshly chopped chives

Heat the chicken stock. Peel and core the pineapple and crush the flesh in a blender or food processor, or chop it finely.

Melt the butter in a saucepan and stir in the flour and cumin to make a roux. Add the stock, stirring and simmering. Mix in the pineapple flesh and set aside to cool. When cold stir in the yogurt, cream, seasoning to taste and coriander and chives. Serve chilled.

Chilled Almond Soup

Serves 4–6

Metric/Imperial	American
1·15 litres/2 pints light stock (veal or chicken)	5 cups light stock (veal or chicken)
1 bouquet garni (celery stick, bay leaf and small sprig of thyme, tied together)	1 bouquet garni (celery stalk, bay leaf and small sprig of thyme, tied together)
225 g/8 oz almonds, blanched	2 cups almonds, blanched
1 clove	1 clove
150 ml/$\frac{1}{4}$ pint yogurt	$\frac{2}{3}$ cup yogurt
2 tablespoons sherry	3 tablespoons sherry
2 drops almond essence	2 dashes almond extract
salt and pepper	salt and pepper

Garnish	Garnish
150 ml/$\frac{1}{4}$ pint double cream	$\frac{2}{3}$ cup heavy cream
1 teaspoon curry powder	1 teaspoon curry powder

Put the stock and bouquet garni on to heat. Crush or grind the almonds, keeping about five aside for splitting for the garnish. Add the ground almonds and clove to the stock and simmer for 10–15 minutes. Remove the bouquet garni and clove and throw them away.

Cool the soup completely then stir in the yogurt, sherry, almond essence and seasoning. Taste for flavour. Whip the cream lightly with the curry powder and float in blobs on the cold almond soup. Finally stick the split almonds into the cream and serve at once.

Friendly Hall Sweet Pepper Soup

Serves 4–5

This used to be served cold in my father's
house in Barbados, but it is also good hot.

Metric/Imperial	**American**
1 onion, peeled and finely chopped	1 onion, peeled and finely chopped
225 g/8 oz green peppers, deseeded and finely chopped	$\frac{1}{2}$ lb green peppers, deseeded and finely chopped
50 g/2 oz butter	$\frac{1}{4}$ cup butter
1 (298-g/10$\frac{1}{2}$-oz) can consommé	1 (10$\frac{1}{2}$-oz) can consommé
1 teaspoon cornflour	1 teaspoon cornstarch
600 ml/1 pint yogurt	2$\frac{1}{2}$ cups yogurt
chopped peppers to garnish	chopped peppers to garnish

Soften the onion and peppers in the butter for a few minutes, without browning. Add the consommé, bring to the boil, then cover and simmer for 10 minutes. Slake the cornflour in a little yogurt and stir into the soup. Continue simmering for 2 minutes to cook the cornflour. Cool and mix in the rest of the yogurt. Garnish with a few chopped peppers on the top.

Diplomat Soup

Serves 6

A chilled soup: this is a tomato and yogurt
cooler from Washington D.C.

Metric/Imperial	**American**
50 g/2 oz butter	$\frac{1}{4}$ cup butter
2 onions, peeled and chopped	2 onions, peeled and chopped
1 medium cucumber, peeled, deseeded and cubed	1 medium cucumber, peeled, deseeded and cubed
2 (396-g/14-oz) cans tomatoes, drained	2 (14-oz) cans tomatoes, drained
freshly chopped basil to taste	freshly chopped basil to taste
300 ml/$\frac{1}{2}$ pint chicken stock	$1\frac{1}{4}$ cups chicken stock
sea salt and freshly ground pepper	coarse salt and freshly ground pepper
300 ml/$\frac{1}{2}$ pint yogurt	$1\frac{1}{4}$ cups yogurt
sprigs of mint to garnish	sprigs of mint to garnish

Melt the butter and gently cook the onions until soft but not brown.
Add the cucumber, tomatoes and basil. Cover and simmer for 10
minutes, then pour in the stock and simmer for a further 10 minutes.
Liquidise in the blender and push through a sieve, discarding any
pips. Cool. Season to taste and stir in yogurt. Chill the soup and
garnish with mint sprigs to serve.

Vichyssoise

This classic soup is actually improved by
replacing the usual cream with yogurt, as it
gives a slightly less bland flavour.

Metric/Imperial	American
4 large leeks, white parts only	4 large leeks, white parts only
1 small onion, peeled and chopped	1 small onion, peeled and chopped
2 tablespoons sunflower oil	3 tablespoons sunflower oil
4 medium potatoes, peeled and sliced	4 medium potatoes, peeled and sliced
600 ml/1 pint chicken stock (fat skimmed off)	$2\frac{1}{2}$ cups chicken stock (fat skimmed off)
sea salt and freshly ground white pepper	coarse salt and freshly ground white pepper
150–300 ml/$\frac{1}{4}$–$\frac{1}{2}$ pint yogurt	$\frac{2}{3}$–$1\frac{1}{4}$ cups yogurt
freshly chopped chives to garnish	freshly chopped chives to garnish

Wash and prepare the leeks carefully, cutting them into rings. Soften with the onion in the oil in a large saucepan, being careful not to let them brown. Add the potatoes and cook gently, stirring, for a further 5 minutes. Add the stock and season sparingly. Cover and cook for 20–30 minutes, until the vegetables are tender. Sieve the soup or liquidise in the blender and allow to cool.

When the soup is cold, stir in the yogurt and serve chilled, with chopped chives floating on top.

For a delicious, more unusual hot soup, omit the potatoes and do not liquidise in a blender, but leave the leeks in rings. A teaspoon of cornflour with the yogurt will prevent it from separating when added to the hot soup. Garnish with chopped parsley to serve.

Nettle Soup

Serves 4

This is a great favourite with my family.
Nettles are full of goodness and free! Only
use the tender young tops of early
summer.

Metric/Imperial

1 small onion, peeled and
chopped
50 g/2 oz butter or
polyunsaturated margarine
1·15 litres/2 pints young nettle
shoots
600 ml/1 pint chicken stock
150 ml/¼ pint yogurt
2 tablespoons single cream
(optional)
sea salt and freshly ground
pepper

American

1 small onion, peeled and
chopped
¼ cup butter or polyunsaturated
margarine
5 cups young nettle shoots
2½ cups chicken stock
⅔ cup yogurt
3 tablespoons light cream
(optional)
coarse salt and freshly ground
pepper

Soften the onion in the butter. Add the nettles and cover the pan.
After a few minutes turn it all about well with a wooden spoon; the
nettles and onion should absorb all the butter. Pour on the stock and
bring to the boil, then cover and simmer gently for about 15 minutes.
Add the yogurt and liquidise in the blender. Reheat and swirl in a little
cream if liked. Taste for seasoning and serve with wholemeal rolls.

Cream of Cauliflower Soup

Serves 8–10

A superb soup, delicate and nourishing.

Metric/Imperial	American
2 tablespoons sunflower oil	3 tablespoons sunflower oil
50 g/2 oz butter or polyunsaturated margarine	$\frac{1}{4}$ cup butter or polyunsaturated margarine
2 medium onions, peeled and finely chopped	2 medium onions, peeled and finely chopped
1 medium carrot, peeled and grated	1 medium carrot, peeled and grated
4 sticks celery, chopped	4 stalks celery, chopped
1 head cauliflower (about 450 g/1 lb), cut into florets	1 head cauliflower (about 1 lb), cut into florets
2 tablespoons freshly chopped parsley	3 tablespoons freshly chopped parsley
40 g/1$\frac{1}{2}$ oz flour	6 tablespoons flour
1·75 litres/3 pints hot chicken stock	7$\frac{1}{2}$ cups hot chicken stock
$\frac{1}{2}$ bay leaf	$\frac{1}{2}$ bay leaf
8 peppercorns	8 peppercorns
300 ml/$\frac{1}{2}$ pint yogurt	1$\frac{1}{4}$ cups yogurt

Heat the oil and butter in a large heavy saucepan. Add the onions, cover and soften, stirring once or twice to make sure they don't catch. Stir in the carrot and celery and cook for a further few minutes. Now add the cauliflower and half the parsley and turn all together with a wooden spoon. Cover and cook gently for 10 minutes. Remove from the heat and sprinkle over the flour. Stir well and then gradually add the hot chicken stock, stirring continuously as each addition comes to the boil. Add the bay leaf and peppercorns, cover the soup and simmer for 15 minutes.

Stir two spoonfuls of soup into the yogurt. Mix the yogurt and the rest of the parsley into the soup. Reheat and serve from a hot tureen.

Starters

This is the curtain raiser course and sets the mood for the whole meal. It can be as simple or extravagant as you please, but should always delight the eye and tempt the palate. Contrast it carefully with the main course so as to avoid monotony of colour, taste or texture.

Yogurt is invaluable as a light, delicate and versatile ingredient in many hors d'oeuvres. Experiment with your own ideas and use it, for example, as the basis for a light mousse or ring mould in which to pile favourite vegetables such as asparagus, or salad ingredients tossed in a light dressing.

Les crudités are a delightfully informal start to a summer meal. Assemble simple raw vegetables in groups on a dish to make a still life painting and serve two or three sauces to dip them in. Eat them with your fingers, and enjoy choosing your favourites.

Prawns and crab meat topped with a cheesy yogurt sauce is a delicious recipe from my friend Moy. Crab soufflé is another lovely dish and makes quite a dramatic start to the meal. Guests should be waiting for the soufflé, and not the soufflé for the guests. Try Arabian Yogurt Appetiser for something really unusual – and Port of Spain Prawns for something exotic – in fact please try them all!

Asparagus Parmesan and Courgette Quiche
(see recipes pages 44 and 45)

Port of Spain Prawns

Serves 4

This is a recipe from Trinidad.

Metric/Imperial	American
2 very small pineapples	2 very small pineapples
4 tablespoons peeled and diced cucumber	$\frac{1}{3}$ cup peeled and diced cucumber
$\frac{1}{2}$ teaspoon salt	$\frac{1}{2}$ teaspoon salt
$\frac{1}{2}$ teaspoon ground cumin	$\frac{1}{2}$ teaspoon ground cumin
$\frac{1}{2}$ teaspoon ground coriander	$\frac{1}{2}$ teaspoon ground coriander
freshly ground black pepper	freshly ground black pepper
150 ml/$\frac{1}{4}$ pint thick yogurt	$\frac{2}{3}$ cup thick yogurt
100 g/4 oz peeled prawns	$\frac{2}{3}$ cup shelled shrimp

Garnish	Garnish
4 unpeeled prawns	4 unshelled shrimp
4 sprigs of watercress or mint	4 sprigs of watercress or mint

Halve the pineapples and remove the cores. Scoop out the flesh, chop it and put in a bowl. Reserve the pineapple shells. Sprinkle the cucumber with the salt and drain in a colander for about 30 minutes. Pat dry. Mix the cumin, coriander, pepper and yogurt together. Add the cucumber to the pineapple and combine with the peeled prawns and the yogurt.

Pile into the four pineapple shells and garnish each with a whole prawn and a sprig of watercress or mint. Serve with brown bread and butter.

Port of Spain Prawns (see recipe above)

Tzatziki

Serves 4

This delicious Greek hors d'oeuvre can be
served on its own, or for a bigger party it
can be joined by bowls of taramasalata
(smoked cod's roe pâté) and aubergine
caviar. Serve with hot pitta bread.

Metric/Imperial	American
$\frac{1}{2}$ medium cucumber	$\frac{1}{2}$ medium cucumber
1 teaspoon salt	1 teaspoon salt
300 ml/$\frac{1}{2}$ pint yogurt	$1\frac{1}{4}$ cups yogurt
1 clove garlic, crushed	1 clove garlic, crushed
freshly ground pepper	freshly ground pepper
1 tablespoon chopped parsley (optional)	1 tablespoon chopped parsley (optional)
Garnish	**Garnish**
lettuce leaves	lettuce leaves
1 bunch mustard and cress	1 bunch mustard or garden cress
1 orange	1 orange

The cucumber can either be peeled and grated or finely diced for this
recipe. Sprinkle with the salt and drain in a colander for 30 minutes.
Pat dry on absorbent paper and then combine with the remaining
ingredients. Chill for 15–20 minutes before serving on a bed of
lettuce leaves, garnished with cress and orange wedges.

Arabian Yogurt Appetiser

Serves 4

This comes from Andrew Gill of Cobbett's
Restaurant, Botley in Hampshire.

Metric/Imperial	American
$\frac{1}{2}$ *medium cucumber, diced*	$\frac{1}{2}$ *medium cucumber, diced*
1 teaspoon salt	*1 teaspoon salt*
300 ml/$\frac{1}{2}$ pint yogurt	*$1\frac{1}{4}$ cups yogurt*
grated rind and juice of $\frac{1}{2}$ lemon	*grated rind and juice of $\frac{1}{2}$ lemon*
100 g/4 oz seedless raisins	*$\frac{3}{4}$ cup seeded raisins*
2 tablespoons chopped walnuts	*3 tablespoons chopped walnuts*
1 hard-boiled egg, chopped	*1 hard-cooked egg, chopped*
1 tablespoon freshly chopped chives	*1 tablespoon freshly chopped chives*

Sprinkle the cucumber with the salt and drain in a colander for about
30 minutes. Pat dry. Combine with the remaining ingredients and
serve in small dishes, with a teaspoon.

Les Crudités

Serves 6–9

A collection of small raw vegetables and
salads assembled in groups on a serving
dish, with bowls of different sauces to
accompany them.

Radishes, baby tomatoes, florets of cauliflower, sticks of celery and
carrot, strips of sweet pepper, rounds of raw courgettes, endive
leaves, baby beetroot (cooked), watercress sprigs, quartered hard-
boiled eggs and tiny new potatoes are all suitable. Wash and dry them
and arrange in groups in an attractive design on a chilled serving dish.
The ingredients can be varied to your own choice.

Each guest should have a plate and also a finger bowl filled with
warm water and a slice of lemon; rose petals add a touch of luxury.
The vegetables are eaten with the fingers. Serve at least three sauces,
in separate bowls; mustard sauce, garlic sauce and anchovy sauce
would be lovely (see pages 87–89). Pass a basket of hot crusty bread,
sea salt and a pepper mill.

Covent Garden Salad

Serves 4

Metric/Imperial	American
6 rashers streaky bacon, rind removed	6 bacon slices, rind removed
2 ripe avocado pears	2 ripe avocados
1 small crisp lettuce	1 small crisp head lettuce

Dressing

6 tablespoons yogurt	$\frac{1}{2}$ cup yogurt
1 tablespoon cider vinegar	1 tablespoon cider vinegar
2 teaspoons lemon juice	2 teaspoons lemon juice
1 teaspoon grated onion	1 teaspoon grated onion
sea salt and freshly ground black pepper	coarse salt and freshly ground black pepper

Cook the rashers of bacon under the grill. Meanwhile, combine the ingredients for the dressing in a bowl, or mix in your blender. Peel the avocados carefully and slice into the yogurt dressing, turning the pieces gently until they are well coated.

Arrange the finely torn lettuce in individual china or glass bowls. Spoon the avocado and dressing on to each and lastly snip the hot bacon over the top.

The hot fat from the bacon is very good poured over too, but avoid this indulgence if you are on a slimming or cholesterol lowering diet.

Serve immediately.

Stuffed Tomatoes

Serves 6

Metric/Imperial	American
6 large tomatoes	6 large tomatoes
2 teaspoons salt	2 teaspoons salt
1 teaspoon castor sugar	1 teaspoon sugar
175 g/6 oz yogurt cheese aux fines herbes (see page 15)	¾ cup yogurt cheese aux fines herbes (see page 15)
2 sticks celery, finely chopped	2 stalks celery, finely chopped
1 tablespoon lemon juice	1 tablespoon lemon juice
2 tablespoons olive or sunflower oil	3 tablespoons olive or sunflower oil
sea salt and freshly ground pepper	coarse salt and freshly ground pepper

Lower the tomatoes into a saucepan of boiling water and take out after 10 seconds. Plunge into cold water and peel them. Slice a lid off the top of each and scoop out the insides with a teaspoon. Sprinkle the insides with the salt and sugar mixed and turn upside down to drain for a few minutes.

Fill the tomatoes with the remaining ingredients, which you have mixed together in a bowl. Serve on a bed of lettuce leaves and hand round a basket of hot bread.

Smoked Mackerel Pâté

Serves 6

This is a no fuss supper party recipe. Serve
it with hot toast and curls of butter. If there
is any left over it will make a lovely filling
for brown bread sandwiches.

Metric/Imperial

450 g/1 lb smoked mackerel
fillets
juice of 1 lemon
150 ml/¼ pint yogurt
freshly ground black pepper
100 g/4 oz unsalted butter,
melted
150 ml/¼ pint double cream,
lightly whipped

Garnish
slices of lemon
sprigs of parsley

American

1 lb smoked mackerel fillets
juice of 1 lemon
⅔ cup yogurt
freshly ground black pepper
½ cup melted unsalted butter
⅔ cup heavy cream, lightly
whipped

Garnish
slices of lemon
sprigs of parsley

Remove the skin from the smoked mackerel fillets. Flake the fish into
a food processor or blender. Add the lemon juice, yogurt, black
pepper and melted butter. Blend these ingredients until smooth and
then quickly blend in the cream. Heap into a dish and smooth over
the top.

Garnish the pâté with lemon slices and parsley sprigs and place in
the refrigerator to set.

Crab Soufflé

Serves 4

Metric/Imperial	**American**
25 g/1 oz butter	2 tablespoons butter
1 tablespoon flour	1 tablespoon flour
150 ml/$\frac{1}{4}$ pint yogurt	$\frac{2}{3}$ cup yogurt
175 g/6 oz crab meat	$\frac{3}{4}$ cup crab meat
4 eggs, separated	4 eggs, separated
salt and freshly ground black pepper	salt and freshly ground black pepper
$\frac{1}{4}$ teaspoon cayenne pepper	$\frac{1}{4}$ teaspoon cayenne pepper

Wipe a butter paper over the base only of a 15-cm/6-inch soufflé dish. Melt the butter and stir in the flour. Add the yogurt, beating with a wooden spoon. Remove from the heat and stir in the crab meat and egg yolks. Season with the salt, pepper and cayenne. Whisk the egg whites into stiff peaks and fold lightly into the crab mixture.

Turn into the soufflé dish and cook in a moderately hot oven (200°C, 400°F, Gas Mark 6) for 18–20 minutes. Serve at once.

Gratin of Seafood

Serves 4–6

Metric/Imperial	American
300 ml/$\frac{1}{2}$ pint yogurt	1$\frac{1}{4}$ cups yogurt
4 eggs, lightly beaten	4 eggs, lightly beaten
1 small onion, peeled and chopped	1 small onion, peeled and chopped
25 g/1 oz butter or polyunsaturated margarine	2 tablespoons butter or polyunsaturated margarine
175 g/6 oz peeled prawns	1 cup shelled shrimp
175 g/6 oz crab meat	$\frac{3}{4}$ cup crab meat
salt and pepper	salt and pepper
2 tablespoons fresh white breadcrumbs	3 tablespoons fresh soft white bread crumbs
2 tablespoons grated Parmesan cheese	3 tablespoons grated Parmesan cheese
25 g/1 oz butter, melted	2 tablespoons melted butter

Beat the yogurt with the eggs. Soften the onion in the butter or margarine and then fold into the yogurt with the seafood. Season lightly to taste. Pour into a gratin dish, or four ramekin dishes, and sprinkle with the breadcrumbs, Parmesan and melted butter.

Place in a roasting tin filled with 5 cm/2 inches of boiling water and cook in a moderately hot oven (190°C, 375°F, Gas Mark 5) for 25–35 minutes, or until set. The timing depends on the dishes used. Serve immediately.

Asparagus Parmesan

Serves 4–6

Metric/Imperial	American
1·5 kg/3 lb fresh or 675 g/1½ lb frozen asparagus	3 lb fresh or 1½ lb frozen asparagus
100 g/4 oz butter	½ cup butter
50 g/2 oz Parmesan cheese, grated	½ cup grated Parmesan cheese
2 tablespoons strong stock	3 tablespoons strong stock
freshly ground pepper	freshly ground pepper
freshly grated nutmeg	freshly grated nutmeg
2 egg yolks	2 egg yolks
1 teaspoon cornflour	1 teaspoon cornstarch
150 ml/¼ pint yogurt	⅔ cup yogurt
grated Parmesan cheese to sprinkle	grated Parmesan cheese to sprinkle

Tie the asparagus in bundles, cut to a uniform length, and cook in boiling salted water for 10–15 minutes, until tender. Cook the frozen asparagus as directed on the packet. Drain and keep warm.

Melt the butter in a saucepan and add the Parmesan, stock, pepper and nutmeg. Stir together until this bubbles. Combine the egg yolks with the cornflour and yogurt. Tip this mixture into the pan, stirring carefully until thoroughly heated, but being careful not to let the eggs scramble. Pour this sauce over the asparagus and serve immediately, sprinkled with Parmesan.

Courgette Quiche

Serves 6

Metric/Imperial	American
350 g/12 oz shortcrust pastry (made with 350 g/12 oz plain flour and 175 g/6 oz fat)	$\frac{3}{4}$ lb basic pie dough (made with 3 cups all-purpose flour and $\frac{3}{4}$ cup shortening)
675 g/1$\frac{1}{2}$ lb courgettes, cut into rings	1$\frac{1}{2}$ lb zucchini, cut into rings
25 g/1 oz butter	2 tablespoons butter
4 eggs	4 eggs
300 ml/$\frac{1}{2}$ pint yogurt	1$\frac{1}{4}$ cups yogurt
sea salt and freshly ground pepper	coarse salt and freshly ground pepper
freshly grated nutmeg	freshly grated nutmeg
50 g/2 oz Parmesan cheese, grated	$\frac{1}{2}$ cup grated Parmesan cheese

Line a 25-cm/10-inch flan ring with the pastry. Cut with scissors about 1 cm/$\frac{1}{2}$ inch above the top of the rim and pinch all round. Prick the base with a fork.

Cook the courgettes for about 10 minutes in boiling salted water. Drain well, pressing down with a plate to squeeze out any excess water. Dot with the butter. Beat the eggs, yogurt, seasoning and a little nutmeg together. Scatter the courgettes in the pastry case, pour over the yogurt and egg mixture and sprinkle with the Parmesan.

Bake the quiche in a moderately hot oven (200°C, 400°F, Gas Mark 6) for 30–40 minutes, until golden and puffy. Serve immediately if possible, though this is almost as good cold.

Note For a crisper pastry, you can bake the pastry case blind for 10 minutes before adding the courgettes. Add the courgette mixture and bake for 30–35 minutes, as above.

Main Course Dishes

Post-war food shortages led to a burst of calvados-and-cream cookery. It was an understandable reaction to austerity, but now the binge is over and there is a marked preference for less fattening, more digestible ingredients. Yogurt can replace cream and soured cream and actually enhance the dish with its piquancy and flavour. Try the Boeuf Stroganoff, briefly cooked steak tossed with onions, peppers and mushrooms, and bathed in a yogurt sauce. Délice de Sole is fillets of sole poached in white wine, finished with a yogurt sauce and topped with lightly browned Parmesan cheese.

Yogurt seems to work equally well with rich dishes and with the more delicate flavours of chicken, veal and fish. Here is a selection of recipes for dinner parties and for the family; I hope you may find some among them that become your favourites too.

Délice de Sole

Serves 4–6

Ask your fishmonger to fillet the sole but to let you have the backbones for the stock.

Metric/Imperial	American
2 sole, filleted	2 sole, filleted
1 small onion, peeled and finely chopped	1 small onion, peeled and finely chopped
300 ml/½ pint dry cider or white wine	1¼ cups dry cider or white wine
salt and pepper	salt and pepper
225 g/8 oz button mushrooms, wiped and sliced	½ lb button mushrooms, wiped and sliced
100 g/4 oz butter or polyunsaturated margarine	½ cup butter or polyunsaturated margarine
juice of ½ lemon	juice of ½ lemon
40 g/1½ oz flour	6 tablespoons flour
300 ml/½ pint yogurt	1¼ cups yogurt
2 tablespoons fresh white breadcrumbs	3 tablespoons fresh white breadcrumbs
2 tablespoons grated Parmesan cheese	3 tablespoons grated Parmesan cheese

Remove and discard the black skin and place the fillets of sole in a large ovenproof dish or roasting tin. Place the onion on top of the sole with the reserved backbones from the fish. Pour in the cider and season. Cover the dish with foil and put into a moderately hot oven (190°C, 375°F, Gas Mark 5) for about 20 minutes, until the fish is cooked. Drain the fish, transfer to a flameproof gratin dish and keep warm. Reserve the liquid and throw away the bones.

Sauté the sliced mushrooms in 75 g/3 oz (U.S. ⅓ cup) butter with the lemon juice. Sprinkle over the flour and stir in. Add the reserved fish liquor, bring to the boil and simmer, stirring continuously. Season to taste. Stir in the yogurt and heat through. Pour this sauce over the fish fillets and sprinkle with breadcrumbs, cheese and the remaining melted butter. Brown under a hot grill and serve at once.

Sherried Lambs' Kidneys

Serves 4

Kidneys are good for you; please don't
hold this against them, but they should be
only briefly and barely cooked.

Metric/Imperial	American
10 lambs' kidneys, skinned and cores removed	10 lamb kidneys, skinned and cores removed
2 tablespoons flour	3 tablespoons flour
2 tablespoons olive oil	3 tablespoons olive oil
50 g/2 oz butter	$\frac{1}{4}$ cup butter
1 teaspoon freshly chopped thyme or $\frac{1}{2}$ teaspoon dried thyme	1 teaspoon freshly chopped thyme or $\frac{1}{2}$ teaspoon dried thyme
2 Spanish onions, peeled and sliced	2 Spanish onions, peeled and sliced
225 g/8 oz small button mushrooms, wiped	$\frac{1}{2}$ lb small button mushrooms, wiped
150 ml/$\frac{1}{4}$ pint medium dry sherry	$\frac{2}{3}$ cup medium dry sherry
150 ml/$\frac{1}{4}$ pint yogurt	$\frac{2}{3}$ cup yogurt
sea salt and freshly ground black pepper	coarse salt and freshly ground black pepper
freshly chopped parsley to garnish	freshly chopped parsley to garnish

Slice the kidneys and toss them in the flour. Heat the oil and butter
with the thyme in a heavy frying pan. Put in the kidneys and fry
quickly for 2–3 minutes to seal them (browned outside with the juices
locked in). Remove with a slotted spoon and set aside in a warm dish.

If necessary add a little more butter and oil to the pan, then soften
the onion, covering the pan with a lid. Add the mushrooms and sauté
for about 4 minutes. Stir in the sherry and continue to cook for a
further 3–4 minutes. Add the yogurt, salt and pepper. Return the
kidneys to the sauce and reheat gently. Serve immediately
with parsley dredged down the centre.

Liver with Sage

Serves 6

This is recollected from Italy, where, thinly sliced and only briefly cooked, liver keeps its delicacy and tenderness. The flavour of the sage marries wonderfully with the liver, onions and yogurt.

Metric/Imperial	American
675 g/1½ lb calf's liver, thinly sliced	1½ lb calf liver, thinly sliced
2 tablespoons flour	3 tablespoons flour
2 tablespoons oil	3 tablespoons oil
50 g/2 oz butter or polyunsaturated margarine	¼ cup butter or polyunsaturated margarine
450 g/1 lb onions, peeled and thinly sliced	1 lb onions, peeled and thinly sliced
300 ml/½ pint yogurt	1¼ cups yogurt
grated rind of 1 lemon	grated rind of 1 lemon
2 tablespoons freshly chopped sage leaves	3 tablespoons freshly chopped sage leaves
salt and freshly ground black pepper	salt and freshly ground black pepper

Sprinkle the liver with the flour and brown briefly on each side in the hot oil and butter. Take out the meat and arrange on a heated serving dish. Keep warm.

Meanwhile, cook the sliced onions in the remaining oil until soft. Mix in the yogurt, lemon rind and sage and heat through, stirring. Season to taste. Pour this sauce over the liver and serve at once.

Lamb and Pepper Kebabs

Serves 4

Metric/Imperial	American
450 g/1 lb shoulder or fillet of lamb	1 lb lamb shoulder or leg steak
1 green pepper	1 green pepper
4 tomatoes	4 tomatoes
2 tablespoons oil	3 tablespoons oil

Marinade	Marinade
300 ml/$\frac{1}{2}$ pint yogurt	$1\frac{1}{4}$ cups yogurt
juice of $\frac{1}{2}$ lemon	juice of $\frac{1}{2}$ lemon
1 clove garlic, crushed	1 clove garlic, crushed
salt and freshly ground pepper	salt and freshly ground pepper
$\frac{1}{2}$ teaspoon dried oregano	$\frac{1}{2}$ teaspoon dried oregano

Remove any fat from the meat and cut into 2·5-cm/1-inch cubes. Deseed the pepper and cut the flesh into small squares. Halve the tomatoes. Mix the yogurt with the lemon juice, garlic, seasoning and oregano, and pour over the lamb. Marinate for 5–6 hours, turning the meat occasionally.

Thread the lamb, peppers and tomatoes on to oiled skewers, sprinkle with oil and grill or barbecue, turning occasionally, for about 20 minutes. Serve with rice and a tossed salad.

Lamb and Pepper Kebabs (see recipe above) and Moussaka (see recipe page 68)

Boeuf Stroganoff

Serves 4

Metric/Imperial	American
450 g/1 lb fillet or good frying steak	1 lb filet mignons or good frying steak
1 medium onion, peeled and finely chopped	1 medium onion, peeled and finely chopped
1 small pepper, deseeded and finely chopped	1 small pepper, deseeded and finely chopped
50 g/2 oz butter or 3 tablespoons oil	$\frac{1}{4}$ cup butter or oil
225 g/8 oz button mushrooms	$\frac{1}{2}$ lb button mushrooms
juice of $\frac{1}{2}$ lemon	juice of $\frac{1}{2}$ lemon
sea salt and freshly ground black pepper	coarse salt and freshly ground black pepper
2 teaspoons cornflour	2 teaspoons cornstarch
300 ml/$\frac{1}{2}$ pint yogurt	$1\frac{1}{4}$ cups yogurt
freshly chopped parsley to garnish	freshly chopped parsley to garnish

Cut the steak into narrow strips, 3·5 cm/$1\frac{1}{2}$ inches long. Cook the onion and green pepper in about half the butter until soft. Wipe the mushrooms and add them to the pan with the lemon juice and seasoning. Simmer for a few minutes. Mix the cornflour with a little yogurt and tip it, with the rest of the yogurt, into the vegetables. Heat through.

Meanwhile heat the remaining butter in a clean sauté pan and cook the steak briefly for about 3–4 minutes, turning once. Serve the steak on a hot serving dish, bathed in the yogurt and vegetable sauce and dredged with parsley.

Note To make the variation illustrated on the jacket, mix the cooked steak with the fried vegetables. Spoon the yogurt over the top and serve on a bed of buttered noodles sprinkled with poppy seeds.

Cold Lemon Chicken (see recipe page 57)

Rabbit with Rosemary and Brandy

Serves 6

This is an elegant and unusual dish;
prepare it with care.

Metric/Imperial	American
1 wild rabbit, jointed	1 wild rabbit, jointed
2 tablespoons sunflower oil	3 tablespoons sunflower oil
50 g/2 oz polyunsaturated margarine or butter	$\frac{1}{4}$ cup polyunsaturated margarine or butter
2 tablespoons flour	3 tablespoons flour
1 large onion, peeled and chopped	1 large onion, peeled and chopped
1 tablespoon freshly chopped rosemary	1 tablespoon freshly chopped rosemary
2 tablespoons brandy	3 tablespoons brandy
2 tablespoons Dijon mustard	3 tablespoons Dijon mustard
300 ml/$\frac{1}{2}$ pint yogurt	$1\frac{1}{4}$ cups yogurt
sea salt and freshly ground pepper	coarse salt and freshly ground pepper

The rabbit should be jointed by your butcher or fishmonger and be a wild one, which has more flavour.

Heat the oil and margarine in a flameproof casserole. Toss the rabbit pieces in the flour and turn them in the oil until lightly browned, then take out and set aside while softening the onion in the remaining oil. Toss in the rosemary and replace the rabbit pieces. Stir in the brandy, mustard and yogurt then cover and simmer very gently for about 30 minutes. Add a little water or stock during cooking if necessary. Season to taste with sea salt and freshly ground pepper.

Serve from the casserole with puréed potatoes and fresh vegetables.

Normandy Chicken

Serves 4

Metric/Imperial	American
50 g/2 oz butter	$\frac{1}{4}$ cup butter
1 (1·5-kg/3$\frac{1}{2}$-lb) chicken	1 (3$\frac{1}{2}$-lb) chicken
2 cooking apples	2 baking apples
3 outer sticks celery	3 outer stalks celery
1 large onion, peeled and sliced	1 large onion, peeled and sliced
$\frac{1}{2}$ teaspoon dried thyme	$\frac{1}{2}$ teaspoon dried thyme
1 tablespoon flour	1 tablespoon flour
300 ml/$\frac{1}{2}$ pint dry white wine or cider	1$\frac{1}{4}$ cups dry white wine or cider
300 ml/$\frac{1}{2}$ pint chicken giblet stock	1$\frac{1}{4}$ cups chicken giblet stock
sea salt and freshly ground pepper	coarse salt and freshly ground pepper
150 ml/$\frac{1}{4}$ pint yogurt	$\frac{2}{3}$ cup yogurt

Garnish

4 dessert apples, peeled	4 dessert apples, peeled
25 g/1 oz butter	2 tablespoons butter
2 tablespoons castor sugar	3 tablespoons sugar
sprigs of watercress	sprigs of watercress

Heat the butter in a flameproof casserole and brown the chicken carefully all over. Peel, core and cut up the apples and clean and chop the celery. Take out the chicken and set aside. Add the onion, apples, thyme and celery to the casserole and cook for 5 minutes. Shake the flour over the mixture and gently stir in the wine or cider and the stock. Season. Return the chicken to the casserole and put on the lid. Simmer gently on top of the stove for 30–40 minutes, or until the chicken is cooked through.

Meanwhile, core the dessert apples and cut into rings. Fry them lightly in the butter and dust with the castor sugar.

Carve the chicken on to a heated serving dish. Add the yogurt to the vegetables in the casserole and heat through. Tip the vegetables and sauce into a sieve and strain over the chicken, mashing the apples and vegetables through as much as possible. Cook the remainder of the head of celery to serve with the chicken. Garnish the chicken with fried apple rings and sprigs of watercress.

Chicken in White Wine

Serves 4

Metric/Imperial	American
2 tablespoons oil	3 tablespoons oil
50 g/2 oz butter or polyunsaturated margarine	$\frac{1}{4}$ cup butter or polyunsaturated margarine
2 medium onions, peeled and thinly sliced	2 medium onions, peeled and thinly sliced
1 (1·5-kg/3–3$\frac{1}{2}$-lb) chicken, jointed	1 (3–3$\frac{1}{2}$-lb) chicken, jointed
225 g/8 oz button mushrooms, wiped and sliced	$\frac{1}{2}$ lb button mushrooms, wiped and sliced
2 tablespoons flour	3 tablespoons flour
2 teaspoons freshly chopped tarragon leaves	2 teaspoons freshly chopped tarragon leaves
350 ml/12 fl oz ($\frac{1}{2}$ bottle) dry white wine	1$\frac{1}{2}$ cups dry white wine
150 ml/$\frac{1}{4}$ pint yogurt	$\frac{2}{3}$ cup yogurt

Heat the oil and butter in a flameproof casserole and cook the onion until soft and golden. Add the chicken pieces and turn occasionally for about 10 minutes over a gentle heat. Add the mushrooms (open ones discolour this dish) and sprinkle the flour on top. Stir everything together gently. Add the tarragon. Pour in the white wine by degrees, bring to the boil, reduce the heat and simmer, covered, for 20 minutes. Add the yogurt towards the end of the cooking time and leave uncovered if the sauce needs to reduce a little.

Cold Lemon Chicken

Serves 6

This makes a lovely buffet dish with leftover stock and vegetables to use for soup the following day.

Metric/Imperial	American
1 (1·75-kg/4-lb) roasting chicken	1 (4-lb) roasting chicken
1 onion, peeled and sliced	1 onion, peeled and sliced
225 g/8 oz carrots, peeled and cut into julienne strips	$\frac{1}{2}$ lb carrots, peeled and cut into julienne strips
1 lemon	1 lemon
salt and white pepper	salt and white pepper
2 egg yolks	2 egg yolks
1 tablespoon cornflour	1 tablespoon cornstarch
300 ml/$\frac{1}{2}$ pint yogurt	$1\frac{1}{4}$ cups yogurt
450 g/1 lb fresh or 225 g/8 oz frozen asparagus, cooked and cooled	1 lb fresh or $\frac{1}{2}$ lb frozen asparagus, cooked and cooled
Garnish	**Garnish**
1 lemon	1 lemon
sprigs of watercress	sprigs of watercress

Place the chicken in a large saucepan with the giblets, onion and carrot. Cover with water, add 2 twists of lemon peel and seasoning, then cover the pan and simmer for 45–55 minutes, until tender. Cool the chicken and remove the flesh from the bones. Cut the meat into bite-sized pieces, discarding any skin.

Blend together about 300 ml/$\frac{1}{2}$ pint (U.S. $1\frac{1}{4}$ cups) of the strained stock with the juice of the lemon, the egg yolks and cornflour. Cook this carefully in a double boiler until the sauce is smooth and coats the back of the wooden spoon. Cool and beat in the yogurt. Thin with a little more chicken stock if necessary and adjust seasoning.

Lay the chicken on a serving dish and mask with the lemon sauce. Arrange the cooked asparagus on top in a lattice pattern, put three wedges of lemon at each corner and garnish with watercress sprigs. Accompany with a tossed green salad, or a selection of salads.

Dishes from Abroad

Yogurt can nowadays be found in kitchens in almost every part of the world, but it originated in the Balkan countries and is part of the ancient cooking traditions of the Near and Middle East. Most of these dishes have evolved from peasant origins and range from simple cooking to the more elaborate preparation of festive food. Yogurt is an essential ingredient in most of these recipes, and is often an important accompaniment to a hot, spicy or 'rich' meal (like the cooling salads of cucumber, yogurt and coriander leaves, so frequently served with Indian and Pakistani curries).

Be sure not to skip the marinating process for delicious tandooris and kormas; the yogurt and spices impart so much tenderness and flavour to the meat and chicken, making the finished dish juicy and succulent. The tandoori oven can be replaced in our modern kitchens by a normal oven, using a chicken brick if you have one, or by a revolving spit.

Bortsch Georgia

Serves 6–8

Metric/Imperial	American
2 raw beetroot, peeled and grated	*2 raw beets, peeled and grated*
2 onions, peeled and chopped	*2 onions, peeled and chopped*
2 large carrots, scraped and grated	*2 large carrots, scraped and grated*
1 parsnip, peeled and grated	*1 parsnip, peeled and grated*
2 leeks, white parts only, washed and chopped	*2 leeks, white parts only, washed and chopped*
1 clove garlic, crushed	*1 clove garlic, crushed*
1 bouquet garni (celery stalk, sprig of thyme and bay leaf, tied together)	*1 bouquet garni (celery stalk, sprig of thyme and bay leaf, tied together)*
2·25 litres/4 pints mutton or ham stock	*5 pints mutton or ham stock*
150 g/5 oz cabbage, shredded	*2 cups shredded cabbage*
3 tomatoes, peeled and chopped	*3 tomatoes, peeled and chopped*
1 teaspoon sugar	*1 teaspoon sugar*
sea salt and freshly ground black pepper	*coarse salt and freshly ground black pepper*
2 tablespoons chopped parsley	*3 tablespoons chopped parsley*
300 ml/$\frac{1}{2}$ pint yogurt	*$1\frac{1}{4}$ cups yogurt*
1 tablespoon flour	*1 tablespoon flour*
150 ml/$\frac{1}{4}$ pint soured cream (optional)	*$\frac{2}{3}$ cup sour cream (optional)*

Put the first seven ingredients into a large pan with the stock. Bring to the boil, cover and simmer for 20 minutes. Now add the cabbage, tomatoes, sugar, seasoning and parsley and cook gently for a further 30 minutes. Work the yogurt and flour together until they are quite smooth. Stir into the soup and cook over a low heat for 5 minutes. Just before serving, swirl in the soured cream.

Tarator

Serves 4–6

This marvellous soup is widely served in
Bulgaria.

Metric/Imperial	*American*
1 medium cucumber, peeled	*1 medium cucumber, peeled*
2 teaspoons salt	*2 teaspoons salt*
1 clove garlic, crushed	*1 clove garlic, crushed*
600 ml/1 pint yogurt	*$2\frac{1}{2}$ cups yogurt*
50 g/2 oz walnuts, finely chopped	*$\frac{1}{2}$ cup finely chopped walnuts*
freshly ground white pepper	*freshly ground white pepper*
freshly chopped parsley or dill leaves to garnish	*freshly chopped parsley or dill leaves to garnish*

Slice the cucumber thickly and then cut into strips. Place in a
colander, sprinkle with the salt and leave over a plate to drain in the
refrigerator for about 30 minutes. Wipe dry with absorbent paper.

Just before serving, mix the cucumber, garlic, yogurt and walnuts.
Season with pepper and serve chilled with finely chopped parsley or
dill sprinkled on top.

Mackerel with Yogurt and Chives

Serves 4

This is one of those simple dishes that is truly excellent. It is a Norwegian recipe, and so is inevitably served with boiled potatoes – very good too! The mackerel must be utterly fresh, with bright eyes and a sparkling silver body.

Metric/Imperial	American
4 mackerel, filleted	4 mackerel, filleted
2 tablespoons flour	3 tablespoons flour
salt and freshly ground black pepper	salt and freshly ground black pepper
3 tablespoons oil	$\frac{1}{4}$ cup oil
300 ml/$\frac{1}{2}$ pint yogurt	$1\frac{1}{4}$ cups yogurt
3 tablespoons freshly chopped chives	$\frac{1}{4}$ cup freshly chopped chives

Dust the mackerel fillets with flour and season with salt and pepper. Fry on each side in the oil in a large pan. When cooked, drain away the oil from the pan. Pour the yogurt and chives over the fish fillets and warm through gently, shuffling the pan, as the fish must not break or stick.

Swedish Meatballs

Serves 4

Metric/Imperial	American
450 g/1 lb minced beef	1 lb ground beef
1 medium onion, peeled and finely chopped	1 medium onion, peeled and finely chopped
1 clove garlic, crushed	1 clove garlic, crushed
$\frac{1}{2}$ teaspoon ground cumin	$\frac{1}{2}$ teaspoon ground cumin
$\frac{1}{4}$ teaspoon dried thyme	$\frac{1}{4}$ teaspoon dried thyme
salt and pepper	salt and pepper
about 50 g/2 oz flour	about $\frac{1}{2}$ cup flour
3 tablespoons sunflower oil	$\frac{1}{4}$ cup sunflower oil
300 ml/$\frac{1}{2}$ pint strong beef stock	$1\frac{1}{4}$ cups strong beef stock
300 ml/$\frac{1}{2}$ pint yogurt	$1\frac{1}{4}$ cups yogurt
$\frac{1}{2}$ teaspoon cayenne pepper	$\frac{1}{2}$ teaspoon cayenne pepper
freshly chopped parsley to garnish	freshly chopped parsley to garnish

Mix the beef with the onion, garlic, cumin, thyme and seasoning in a bowl. Shape into smallish balls and dust with flour. Fry the meatballs in the oil until golden brown, then remove with a slotted spoon and drain on absorbent paper.

Stir the remaining flour into the fat left in the pan. Add the stock, bring to the boil, stirring constantly, and simmer until smooth and thickened. Mix in the yogurt. Return the meatballs to the sauce and add the cayenne and seasoning to taste. Transfer to an ovenproof casserole and cook, covered, in a moderate oven (180°C, 350°F, Gas Mark 4) for 30 minutes.

Serve with parsley dusted on the top and accompany with boiled potatoes and a dish of redcurrant jelly.

Veal Creole Style

Serves 6

Metric/Imperial	American
1·75 kg/4 lb breast of veal	4 lb breast of veal
3 tablespoons flour	$\frac{1}{4}$ cup flour
100 g/4 oz butter	$\frac{1}{2}$ cup butter
1 large Spanish onion, peeled and chopped	1 large Spanish onion, peeled and chopped
1 (793-g/1 lb 12-oz) can tomatoes	1 (28-oz) can tomatoes
2 small chilli peppers, sliced	2 small chili peppers, sliced
twist of lemon peel	twist of lemon peel
1 tablespoon curry powder	1 tablespoon curry powder
1 bay leaf	1 bay leaf
2 teaspoons freshly chopped thyme	2 teaspoons freshly chopped thyme
600 ml/1 pint light stock	$2\frac{1}{2}$ cups light stock
2 cloves garlic, crushed	2 cloves garlic, crushed
salt and pepper	salt and pepper
300 ml/$\frac{1}{2}$ pint yogurt	$1\frac{1}{4}$ cups yogurt
1 tablespoon cornflour	1 tablespoon cornstarch
freshly chopped parsley to garnish	freshly chopped parsley to garnish

Trim the meat, discarding any fat, and cut into 4-cm/1$\frac{1}{2}$-inch cubes. Dust with the flour. Heat the butter in a flameproof casserole and brown the veal all over. Remove the meat and cook the onion until softened. Return the meat to the casserole with the tomatoes, chillies, lemon peel, curry powder, bay leaf, thyme and stock. Cover and simmer gently for 1 hour. Stir in the crushed garlic with seasoning to taste and cook for a further hour.

Just before serving, mix the yogurt with the cornflour and mix in. Cook, stirring, for a few minutes. Dust the top with parsley and serve with rice.

Hungarian Pork Paprika

Serves 6–8

Originally cooked by shepherds in a pot over an open fire, the gulyás later became adapted to the sophisticated tastes of the Hapsburg court. Today the gulyás (goulash) can be a glorious spicy stew or a delicately flavoured dish, fit for an archduke! Traditional accompaniments are buttered noodles, lescó (a spicy ratatouille made with bacon and paprika), long-grain rice, and little balls of cucumber which have been sautéed in butter, bathed in warm yogurt and dusted with salt and pepper.

Metric/Imperial	American
75 g/3 oz butter or 4/5 tablespoons oil	$\frac{1}{3}$ cup butter or oil
1 large onion, peeled and chopped	1 large onion, peeled and chopped
1 clove garlic, crushed	1 clove garlic, crushed
1 kg/2 lb pork tenderloin	2 lb pork tenderloin
2 tablespoons flour, seasoned with salt and pepper	3 tablespoons flour, seasoned with salt and pepper
2 tablespoons paprika pepper	3 tablespoons paprika pepper
4 medium tomatoes, peeled, deseeded and chopped	4 medium tomatoes, peeled, deseeded and chopped
1 green pepper, deseeded and diced	1 green pepper, deseeded and diced

Metric/Imperial	American
1 teaspoon sea salt	1 teaspoon coarse salt
$1\frac{1}{2}$ teaspoons cornflour	$1\frac{1}{2}$ teaspoons cornstarch
300 ml/$\frac{1}{2}$ pint yogurt	$1\frac{1}{4}$ cups yogurt
150 ml/$\frac{1}{4}$ pint soured cream	$\frac{2}{3}$ cup sour cream
freshly chopped parsley to garnish	freshly chopped parsley to garnish

Heat the butter or oil in a flameproof casserole and sauté the onion and garlic. Cut the pork into 2·5-cm/1-inch cubes, toss in the flour and stir into the onion, continuing to sauté for about 10 minutes. Add the paprika and mix well. Stir in the tomatoes, green pepper and salt. Pour in a little warm water to almost cover. Place a lid on the casserole and continue to simmer very gently for 1 hour. Check occasionally to see that the liquid has not evaporated and to give the meat a stir.

Mix the cornflour with a little of the yogurt and then add the rest of the yogurt. Pour this gradually into the gulyás, stirring and simmering for a minute or two. Add the soured cream and heat carefully, but do not boil. Dust with parsley to serve.

Lamb Korma

Serves 6

Metric/Imperial	American
1·5 kg/3 lb boneless lamb, shoulder or leg	3 lb boneless lamb, shoulder or leg
300 ml/½ pint yogurt	1¼ cups yogurt
5-cm/2-inch piece of fresh root ginger, peeled and finely chopped	2-inch piece of fresh ginger root, peeled and finely chopped
seeds of 6 cardamom pods	seeds of 6 cardamom pods
1½ teaspoons ground cumin	1½ teaspoons ground cumin
½ teaspoon turmeric powder	½ teaspoon turmeric powder
100 g/4 oz freshly grated or desiccated coconut	1⅓ cups shredded coconut
300 ml/½ pint water	1¼ cups water
6 tablespoons oil, or 100 g/4 oz butter or ghee, melted	½ cup oil, butter or ghee, melted
2 Spanish onions, peeled and chopped	2 Spanish onions, peeled and chopped
2 cloves garlic, crushed	2 cloves garlic, crushed
salt and freshly ground black pepper	salt and freshly ground black pepper
½ teaspoon cayenne pepper	½ teaspoon cayenne pepper
1 cinnamon stick	1 cinnamon stick
4 cloves	4 cloves
3 tomatoes, peeled and quartered	3 tomatoes, peeled and quartered
juice of ½ lemon	juice of ½ lemon

Trim any excess fat off the meat and cut into 2·5-cm/1-inch cubes. Mix the yogurt with the ginger, crushed cardamom seeds, cumin and turmeric. Turn the lamb pieces in this marinade in a bowl, cover and leave in a cool place for 6 hours.

Meanwhile, simmer the coconut in the water for 15 minutes. Strain and reserve the liquor.

Heat the oil in a large frying pan and fry the onions and garlic until soft and golden. Add the lamb and its marinade and fry, stirring, for about 5 minutes. Mix in the salt, pepper and cayenne and add the cinnamon stick and cloves. Stir in the tomatoes and coconut liquor. Bring gently back to the boil, cover and simmer for about 1 hour. Remove the lid if the sauce needs to reduce a little. At the end of the cooking time remove the cinnamon stick and cloves. Finally adjust seasoning to taste and add the lemon juice.

Serve with rice and the usual side dishes that go with curry; quartered tomatoes, sliced raw onion, mango chutney, poppadoms, banana slices tossed in lemon juice, parsley and raita. Raita is a salad from Northern India, a dish made from yogurt and with cool fresh additions of fruit or vegetables (such as diced peeled cucumber) and fresh herbs, especially chopped coriander and mint leaves. Another variation is yogurt with 2 chopped chillies added (seeds removed and discarded first).

Moussaka

Serves 4

Metric/Imperial	American
3 aubergines	3 eggplant
2 teaspoons salt	2 teaspoons salt
2 onions, peeled and chopped	2 onions, peeled and chopped
2 cloves garlic, crushed	2 cloves garlic, crushed
150 ml/$\frac{1}{4}$ pint olive oil	$\frac{2}{3}$ cup olive oil
450 g/1 lb minced lamb	1 lb ground lamb
4 tomatoes, peeled	4 tomatoes, peeled
1 teaspoon dried oregano	1 teaspoon dried oregano
freshly grated nutmeg	freshly grated nutmeg
4 tablespoons red wine	$\frac{1}{3}$ cup red wine
sea salt and freshly ground black pepper	coarse salt and freshly ground black pepper
300 ml/$\frac{1}{2}$ pint yogurt	1$\frac{1}{4}$ cups yogurt
600 ml/1 pint béchamel sauce (made with 50 g/2 oz butter, 50 g/2 oz flour and 600 ml/ 1 pint milk)	2$\frac{1}{2}$ cups béchamel sauce (made with $\frac{1}{4}$ cup butter, $\frac{1}{2}$ cup flour and 2$\frac{1}{2}$ cups milk)
3 eggs	3 eggs
50 g/2 oz Parmesan cheese, grated	$\frac{1}{2}$ cup grated Parmesan cheese

Slice the aubergines, sprinkle with the salt and leave to drain in a colander for 30 minutes.

Meanwhile, make a meat sauce. Cook the onion and garlic in 1$\frac{1}{2}$ tablespoons (U.S. 2 tablespoons) oil. Add the lamb, tomatoes, oregano, nutmeg, red wine and seasoning and simmer, uncovered, for 30 minutes. Mix the yogurt into the béchamel sauce and season to taste. Fold 150 ml/$\frac{1}{4}$ pint (U.S. $\frac{2}{3}$ cup) of this sauce into the meat.

Rinse and dry the aubergines and fry in the remaining oil, a few at a time, until golden on both sides. Layer the aubergines and meat sauce (beginning and ending with aubergines) into a large shallow ovenproof dish. Beat the eggs into the remaining béchamel sauce and pour over all. Sprinkle the Parmesan and a few drops of oil on top. Bake in a moderately hot oven (190°C, 375°F, Gas Mark 5) for 40 minutes, or until golden and bubbling.

Tandoori Chicken

Serves 4

Metric/Imperial	American
1 (1·5-kg/3-lb) chicken	1 (3-lb) chicken
sea salt and freshly ground black pepper	coarse salt and freshly ground black pepper
juice of 1 lemon	juice of 1 lemon
2 tablespoons oil or 40 g/1½ oz butter or ghee, melted	3 tablespoons oil, butter or ghee, melted

Marinade	Marinade
2 cloves garlic, crushed	2 cloves garlic, crushed
1½ teaspoons ground cumin	1½ teaspoons ground cumin
1 teaspoon ground coriander	1 teaspoon ground coriander
150 ml/¼ pint yogurt	⅔ cup yogurt
5-cm/2-inch piece of fresh root ginger, peeled and finely chopped	2-inch piece of fresh ginger root, peeled and finely chopped
½ teasooon cayenne pepper	½ teaspoon cayenne pepper
few drops red vegetable colouring	few dashes red vegetable coloring

Rinse the chicken and pat it dry. Make diagonal cuts on the breast and thigh meat. Rub the chicken all over with the salt, pepper and lemon juice and stand in a bowl while preparing the marinade.

Blend together all the ingredients for the marinade and turn the chicken in this mixture. Cover and leave in the refrigerator for 24 hours, turning the chicken occasionally and spooning the marinade mixture over it.

Place the chicken on a rack in a roasting tin, spoon over the marinade and sprinkle with the oil or melted butter. Roast in a moderately hot oven (200°C, 400°F, Gas Mark 6) for 1¼ hours. Do not baste during the last 15 minutes. Serve hot, accompanied with rice and a dish of vegetables in sauce.

Spiced Chicken

Serves 4–6

Metric/Imperial	American
75 g/3 oz butter	$\frac{1}{3}$ cup butter
4–6 chicken breasts, skinned	4–6 chicken breasts, skinned
1$\frac{1}{2}$ tablespoons flour	2 tablespoons flour
3 onions, peeled and chopped	3 onions, peeled and chopped
1 clove garlic, crushed	1 clove garlic, crushed
2 teaspoons each of ground ginger, paprika pepper and sugar	2 teaspoons each of ground ginger, paprika pepper and sugar
4 cloves	4 cloves
10-cm/4-inch cinnamon stick	4-inch cinnamon stick
2 bay leaves	2 bay leaves
salt and pepper	salt and pepper
300 ml/$\frac{1}{2}$ pint stock or water	1$\frac{1}{4}$ cups stock or water
150 ml/$\frac{1}{4}$ pint yogurt	$\frac{2}{3}$ cup yogurt

Melt the butter in a sauté pan and lightly brown the chicken pieces tossed in flour. Take them out and add the onion, garlic, spices, sugar, bay leaves and seasoning. Cook to soften the onion and bring out the flavours. Return the chicken to the pan, add the stock then cover and simmer for about 20 minutes.

Just before serving, stir in the yogurt. Remove the cinnamon stick and cloves and serve accompanied with rice.

Poulet Fromage Blanc

Serves 4–6

Metric/Imperial	American
grated rind and juice of 1 lemon	grated rind and juice of 1 lemon
175 g/6 oz fromage blanc (see page 16)	¾ cup fromage blanc (see page 16)
sea salt and freshly ground pepper	coarse salt and freshly ground pepper
1 (1·5–1·75 kg/3½–4 lb) chicken	1 (3½–4-lb) chicken
50 g/2 oz butter or polyunsaturated margarine	¼ cup butter or polyunsaturated margarine
2 teaspoons freshly chopped tarragon leaves	2 teaspoons freshly chopped tarragon leaves

Stir the lemon rind into the fromage blanc with seasoning to taste. Stuff the chicken with this. Lay the bird in a roasting tin and surround with the giblets. Butter the chicken all over, sprinkle with tarragon and pour a cup of water and the lemon juice into the tin. Cover with a couple of butter papers and roast in a moderately hot oven (200°C, 400°F, Gas Mark 6) for 1¼ hours, or until cooked. The leg joints should move easily. Scoop some of the creamy stuffing out with a spoon and put into the tin. Take up the bird and carve on to a hot dish. Stir the pan juices and strain into a sauceboat.

Serve the chicken with its lemony cheese stuffing and the juices poured over. Delicious!

Coeur
à la Crème

Serves 4

Metric/Imperial	American
225 g/8 oz yogurt cheese (see page 15)	1 cup yogurt cheese (see page 15)
300 ml/$\frac{1}{2}$ pint soured cream (or whipped cream)	1$\frac{1}{4}$ cups sour cream (or whipped heavy cream)
2 tablespoons castor sugar	3 tablespoons superfine sugar
2 egg whites	2 egg whites
150 ml/$\frac{1}{4}$ pint thick yogurt	$\frac{2}{3}$ cup thick yogurt
100 g/4 oz wild strawberries (or 100 g/4 oz redcurrant jelly)	$\frac{1}{2}$ cup wild strawberries (or $\frac{1}{2}$ cup redcurrant jelly)

Beat the yogurt cheese and soured cream together until smooth. Now beat in the castor sugar. Whisk the egg whites until they stand in stiff peaks and fold them in carefully with a metal spoon.

Line four individual heart-shaped, perforated moulds with muslin and turn the mixture into them. Drain overnight in a cool place, using a large dish underneath to catch the drips.

Turn out and serve with a little thick yogurt spooned over, and sprinkle with tiny wild strawberries or sieved redcurrant jelly piped from a forcing bag.

Note Before preparing this dessert, wring out the muslin in cold water with a tablespoon of fresh lemon juice and $\frac{1}{2}$ teaspoon bicarbonate of soda added.

Supper Dishes

These are light and tempting no-fuss recipes which include salads and vegetable dishes and a selection of rice, pasta and other favourites.

Keep a bowl of fresh yogurt in your refrigerator to make easy and delicious desserts, and quick sauces for vegetables. Try warming a sauceboat of yogurt with chopped chives to serve with baked jacket potatoes; or take the tops off the potatoes, scoop out some of the inside and pour in yogurt mixed with cumin seeds. Replace the lids and put the potatoes back in the oven until you are ready to eat them. This is especially good with steak and salad, and is a new and interesting flavour combination.

Do plan now to sow plenty of seeds in the spring for a good supply of herbs. Fresh dill, chives, tarragon and mint combine beautifully with yogurt to enhance salads, fish and delicious vegetables in season.

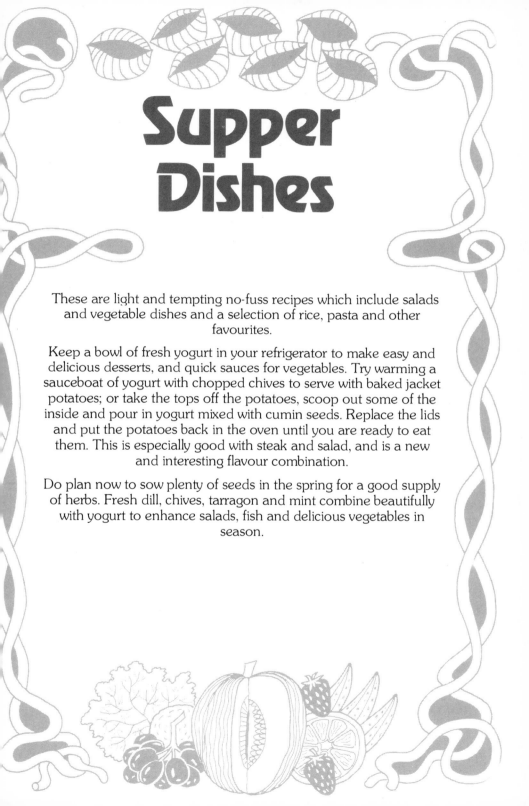

Cheat's Chicken Pie

Serves 6

This is delicious, which is more than it
deserves. It was invented for sly, lazy
cooks. Keep it a secret!

Metric/Imperial	**American**
6 chicken breasts or chicken pieces	*6 chicken breasts or chicken pieces*
75 g/3 oz butter	*6 tablespoons butter*
1 (298-g/10½-oz) can condensed mushroom soup	*1 (10½-oz) can condensed mushroom soup*
150 ml/¼ pint yogurt	*⅔ cup yogurt*
2 tablespoons sherry	*3 tablespoons sherry*
salt and freshly ground pepper	*salt and freshly ground pepper*
6 slices buttered bread	*6 slices buttered bread*

Fry the chicken pieces in the butter until cooked. Arrange all in a
shallow ovenproof dish. Mix the soup with the yogurt and sherry,
season to taste and pour over the chicken. Lay the bread slices on
top, butter side up. Bake in a moderately hot oven (200°C, 400°F,
Gas Mark 6) for 15–20 minutes, until the bread is golden.

Eat with a salad.

Chicken Livers with Brown Rice

Serves 4

Metric/Imperial	American
150 g/5 oz brown rice, soaked for 30 minutes	$\frac{2}{3}$ cup brown rice, soaked for 30 minutes
1 medium onion, peeled and sliced	1 medium onion, peeled and sliced
2 tablespoons sunflower oil	3 tablespoons sunflower oil
50 g/2 oz butter	$\frac{1}{4}$ cup butter
225 g/8 oz chicken livers, trimmed	$\frac{1}{2}$ lb chicken livers, trimmed
225 g/8 oz tomatoes, peeled and sliced	$\frac{1}{2}$ lb tomatoes, peeled and sliced
100 g/4 oz frozen petits pois, cooked	$\frac{3}{4}$ cup frozen petits pois, cooked
150 ml/$\frac{1}{4}$ pint yogurt	$\frac{2}{3}$ cup yogurt
2 tablespoons freshly chopped herbs (parsley, thyme, chervil, tarragon)	3 tablespoons freshly chopped herbs (parsley, thyme, chervil, tarragon)
salt and freshly ground black pepper	salt and freshly ground black pepper
1 lemon, quartered, to garnish	1 lemon, quartered, to garnish

Cook the rice for about 40 minutes in plenty of boiling salted water. Drain and keep warm with a damp tea towel on top.

Sauté the onion in the oil and butter, then add the chicken livers, roughly sliced. Cook for about 2 minutes. Stir in the tomatoes and cook for a further 2–3 minutes. Combine with the hot rice and all the remaining ingredients. Transfer to a hot serving dish and garnish with lemon quarters.

Spaghetti with Mushrooms

Serves 6

Metric/Imperial	American
450 g/1 lb spaghetti	1 lb spaghetti
2 tablespoons olive oil	3 tablespoons olive oil
sea salt and freshly ground black pepper	coarse salt and freshly ground black pepper
225 g/8 oz button mushrooms, wiped and sliced	$\frac{1}{2}$ lb button mushrooms, wiped and sliced
100 g/4 oz butter	$\frac{1}{2}$ cup butter
1 tablespoon flour	1 tablespoon flour
150 ml/$\frac{1}{4}$ pint dry white wine	$\frac{2}{3}$ cup dry white wine
300 ml/$\frac{1}{2}$ pint yogurt	$1\frac{1}{4}$ cups yogurt
3 egg yolks	3 egg yolks
3 tablespoons freshly chopped chives	$\frac{1}{4}$ cup freshly chopped chives

Boil the spaghetti fast in a large pan of salted water for approximately 10 minutes. Drain and toss in the olive oil, seasoning to taste.

Meanwhile, sauté the mushrooms in the butter. Sprinkle on the flour, stir in the wine and cook for a few minutes. Blend the yogurt with the egg yolks, chives and seasoning. Add carefully to the pan. Heat through, stirring with a wooden spoon, without allowing the egg yolks to curdle. Serve immediately, tossed into or poured over the pasta. Sprinkle with extra chopped chives, if liked.

Conchiglie Salad

Serves 4

This makes a lovely accompaniment to
cold roast duck.

Metric/Imperial	American
225 g/8 oz pasta shells	$\frac{1}{2}$ lb pasta shells
2 tablespoons olive or sunflower oil	3 tablespoons olive or sunflower oil
1$\frac{1}{2}$ teaspoons wine vinegar	1$\frac{1}{2}$ teaspoons wine vinegar
salt and freshly ground pepper	salt and freshly ground pepper
2 oranges, peel and pith removed	2 oranges, peel and pith removed
1 green pepper, deseeded and chopped	1 green pepper, deseeded and chopped
4–6 rashers streaky bacon, rind removed, chopped and fried	4–6 bacon slices, rind removed, chopped and fried
300 ml/$\frac{1}{2}$ pint yogurt	1$\frac{1}{4}$ cups yogurt
Garnish	*Garnish*
1 lettuce	1 head lettuce
sprigs of watercress	sprigs of watercress

Cook the pasta in boiling salted water for about 10 minutes. Drain and toss in the oil and vinegar. Season, adding plenty of pepper, and allow to cool. Cut the oranges lengthways into the centre to free the segments from the membrane.

Toss all the ingredients lightly together and pile up the salad in a roomy dish. Surround with lettuce leaves and place a posy of watercress in the centre.

Norwegian Salad

Serves 4

Metric/Imperial
2–4 pickled herring fillets
4 small beetroot, cooked, peeled and diced
8 small new potatoes, scraped, cooked and diced
1 (200-g/7-oz) can pineapple cubes
1 pickled dill cucumber
300 ml/½ pint thick yogurt
2 tablespoons freshly chopped chives

American
2–4 pickled herring fillets
4 small beets, cooked, peeled and diced
8 small new potatoes, scraped, cooked and diced
1 (7-oz) can pineapple cubes
1 dill pickle
1¼ cups thick yogurt
3 tablespoons freshly chopped chives

Slice the pickled herring fillets into bite-sized chunks. Combine in a bowl with the diced beetroot and potato, drained pineapple cubes and chunks of pickled cucumber. Turn out on to a serving dish and pour the yogurt over all. Scatter chives on the top and chill before serving.

Virgin Island's Salad

Metric/Imperial	American
1 lettuce	1 head lettuce
100 g/4 oz yogurt cheese (see page 15) or curd cheese	$\frac{1}{2}$ cup yogurt cheese (see page 15) or curd cheese
1 tablespoon chopped peanuts	1 tablespoon chopped peanuts
2 bananas	2 bananas
2 teaspoons lime or lemon juice	2 teaspoons lime or lemon juice
150 ml/$\frac{1}{4}$ pint yogurt	$\frac{2}{3}$ cup yogurt
2 fresh peaches	2 fresh peaches

Wash the lettuce and arrange on four plates. Shape the cheese into balls about the size of a walnut and roll in the chopped peanuts. Place the cheese balls on the lettuce leaves and add sliced bananas, sprinkled with lime or lemon juice. Pour over the yogurt and arrange sliced, unpeeled peaches on the top.

Healthnut Special

Serves 4

Fresh fruit with yogurt, sweetened with
honey and sprinkled with energising
wheatgerm. This originates from Bermuda.

Metric/Imperial	*American*
1 lettuce heart, washed and dried	1 head lettuce, washed and dried
1 small melon	1 small melon
1 orange	1 orange
1 pink-fleshed Texan grapefruit	1 pink-fleshed Texan grapefruit
225 g/8 oz black grapes	$\frac{1}{2}$ lb purple grapes
100 g/4 oz strawberries, halved	$\frac{1}{4}$ lb strawberries, halved
300 ml/$\frac{1}{2}$ pint yogurt	$1\frac{1}{4}$ cups yogurt
2 tablespoons runny honey	3 tablespoons runny honey
100 g/4 oz toasted wheatgerm	1 cup toasted wheatgerm

Shred the lettuce and lay some over the bottom of each plate. Divide
the melon into eight, removing and discarding the pips and skin.
Place two slices on each plate. Peel the skin and pith off the orange
and grapefruit and cut down in segments towards the centre, leaving
the membrane behind.

Divide all the fruit between the four plates, keeping each type of
fruit separate. Pour over the yogurt, drizzle on honey and sprinkle the
crunchy wheatgerm separately.

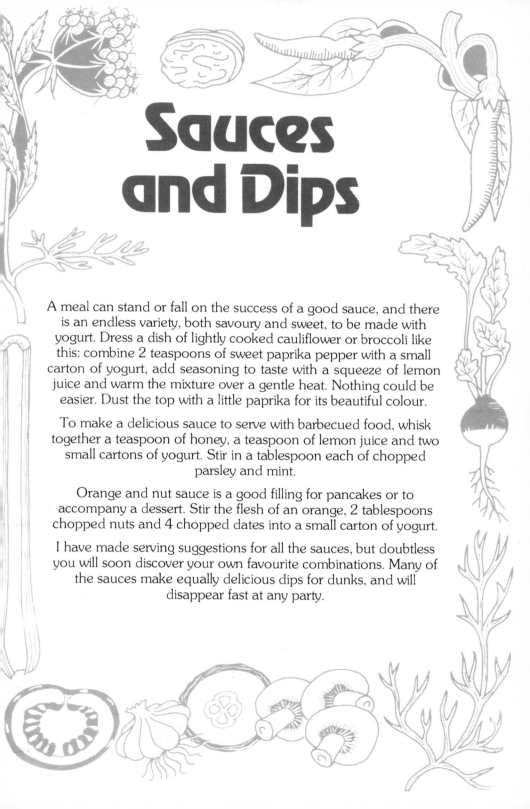

Sauces and Dips

A meal can stand or fall on the success of a good sauce, and there is an endless variety, both savoury and sweet, to be made with yogurt. Dress a dish of lightly cooked cauliflower or broccoli like this: combine 2 teaspoons of sweet paprika pepper with a small carton of yogurt, add seasoning to taste with a squeeze of lemon juice and warm the mixture over a gentle heat. Nothing could be easier. Dust the top with a little paprika for its beautiful colour.

To make a delicious sauce to serve with barbecued food, whisk together a teaspoon of honey, a teaspoon of lemon juice and two small cartons of yogurt. Stir in a tablespoon each of chopped parsley and mint.

Orange and nut sauce is a good filling for pancakes or to accompany a dessert. Stir the flesh of an orange, 2 tablespoons chopped nuts and 4 chopped dates into a small carton of yogurt.

I have made serving suggestions for all the sauces, but doubtless you will soon discover your own favourite combinations. Many of the sauces make equally delicious dips for dunks, and will disappear fast at any party.

Curry Sauce

Makes about 450 ml/¾ pint (U.S. 2 cups)

This basic curry sauce is good with fish,
meat, egg and vegetable dishes.

Metric/Imperial	American
1 onion, peeled and chopped	1 onion, peeled and chopped
50 g/2 oz butter	¼ cup butter
1 clove garlic, crushed	1 clove garlic, crushed
2 chilli peppers, finely chopped	2 chili peppers, finely chopped
2·5-cm/1-inch piece of fresh root ginger, peeled and finely chopped	1-inch piece of fresh ginger root, peeled and finely chopped
2 teaspoons cumin seeds	2 teaspoons cumin seeds
2 teaspoons ground coriander	2 teaspoons ground coriander
½ teaspoon turmeric powder	½ teaspoon turmeric powder
1 teaspoon salt	1 teaspoon salt
1 clove	1 clove
3 tomatoes, peeled and chopped	3 tomatoes, peeled and chopped
freshly ground black pepper	freshly ground black pepper
300 ml/½ pint yogurt	1¼ cups yogurt
1½ teaspoons cornflour	1½ teaspoons cornstarch

Sauté the onion in the butter with the garlic, chillies and ginger.
Prepare the spice paste by putting the cumin, coriander, turmeric, salt
and clove into your blender with a little water. When blended, add to
the sauté pan and cook for 5 minutes. Now stir in the tomatoes and
pepper, and the yogurt mixed with the cornflour. Simmer gently for
10–15 minutes. Add a little hot water if the sauce is too thick.

Mushroom Sauce

Makes about 600 ml/1 pint (U.S. 2½ cups)

This is a good accompaniment for fish,
chicken and veal dishes.

Metric/Imperial	American
1 small onion, peeled and chopped	1 small onion, peeled and chopped
75 g/3 oz butter	⅓ cup butter
225 g/8 oz button mushrooms, wiped and sliced	½ lb button mushrooms, wiped and sliced
juice of ½ lemon	juice of ½ lemon
2 tablespoons flour	3 tablespoons flour
300 ml/½ pint dry cider or white wine	1¼ cups dry cider or white wine
½ teaspoon Worcestershire sauce	½ teaspoon Worcestershire sauce
salt and pepper	salt and pepper
300 ml/½ pint yogurt	1¼ cups yogurt

Soften the onion in the butter and add the mushrooms and lemon
juice. Shake over the flour and stir in for a minute or two. Gradually
add the cider or wine, stirring all the time, and bring to the boil.
Season with Worcestershire sauce, salt and pepper. Simmer for a few
minutes and stir in the yogurt just before serving.

Seafood Sauce

Makes just under 450 ml/¾ pint (U.S. scant 2 cups)

This is simple to prepare and is ideal for
serving with all types of shellfish to make
an excellent starter.

Metric/Imperial	American
2 tablespoons mayonnaise	*3 tablespoons mayonnaise*
2 teaspoons tomato purée	*2 teaspoons tomato paste*
juice of ½ lemon	*juice of ½ lemon*
300 ml/½ pint yogurt	*1¼ cups yogurt*
1 teaspoon Worcestershire sauce	*1 teaspoon Worcestershire sauce*
5 drops Tabasco sauce	*5 dashes Tabasco sauce*
salt and pepper	*salt and pepper*
1 tablespoon chopped capers	*1 tablespoon chopped capers*
1 tablespoon freshly chopped chives	*1 tablespoon freshly chopped chives*

Stir and combine all the ingredients together, and allow to stand for a
few hours in the refrigerator before serving.

*Spaghetti with Mushrooms and Conchiglie
Salad (see recipes pages 76 and 77)*

Mustard Sauce

Makes about 300 ml/½ pint (U.S. 1¼ cups)

This is excellent with all sausage, pork and ham dishes, as well as an accompaniment to crudités. It is also a good sauce to serve with mackerel and herring.

Metric/Imperial	*American*
2 tablespoons Dijon mustard	*3 tablespoons Dijon mustard*
150 ml/¼ pint yogurt	*⅔ cup yogurt*
150 ml/¼ pint thick mayonnaise	*⅔ cup thick mayonnaise*

Whizz this sauce in your blender or food processor, or beat together with a rotary whisk in a bowl. Turn out into a small bowl.

*Crudités (see page 38) with Mustard Sauce
(see recipe above), Garlic Sauce and
Anchovy Sauce (see recipes overleaf)*

Garlic Sauce

Makes about 225 ml/7½ fl oz (U.S. scant 1 cup)

Serve this sauce as a dunk for raw
vegetables.

Metric/Imperial	*American*
2 cloves garlic, crushed	*2 cloves garlic, crushed*
150 g/5 oz yogurt cheese aux	*scant ⅔ cup yogurt cheese aux*
fines herbes (see page 15)	*fines herbes (see page 15)*
2 teaspoons lemon juice	*2 teaspoons lemon juice*
3 tablespoons yogurt	*¼ cup yogurt*
½ teaspoon celery salt	*½ teaspoon celery salt*

Liquidise in the blender or food processor, or work together with a
wooden spoon in a mixing bowl. Serve from a small bowl.

Anchovy Sauce

Makes about 250 ml/8 fl oz (U.S. 1 cup)

Lovely as a dip with crudités
(see page 38).

Metric/Imperial	American
1 (56-g/2-oz) can anchovy fillets, soaked in milk	1 (2-oz) can anchovy fillets, soaked in milk
150 g/5 oz yogurt cheese (see page 15) or cottage cheese	scant $\frac{2}{3}$ cup yogurt cheese (see page 15) or cottage cheese
2 teaspoons lemon juice	2 teaspoons lemon juice
5 drops Tabasco sauce (optional)	5 dashes Tabasco sauce (optional)
3 tablespoons yogurt	$\frac{1}{4}$ cup yogurt

Liquidise in a blender or food processor, or work the ingredients, in the order listed, with a wooden spoon, until you have obtained a smooth sauce.

Dill Sauce

Makes about 300 ml/½ pint (U.S. 1¼ cups)

It is well worth planting a packet of dill seed in your garden every year for this delicious herb which the Scandinavians love so. It is a pretty feathery plant which looks very much like fennel but has a totally different flavour. Use it in salads, on potatoes, with fish and in a velouté sauce for boiled leg of lamb.

The following sauce is excellent with pickled or marinated herring. Soak the herring fillets first if they are too strong.

Metric/Imperial	American
150 ml/¼ pint yogurt	⅔ cup yogurt
150 ml/¼ pint soured cream	⅔ cup sour cream
1 teaspoon Dijon mustard	1 teaspoon Dijon mustard
2 teaspoons grated onion	2 teaspoons grated onion
4 tablespoons freshly chopped dill	⅓ cup freshly chopped dill
sea salt and freshly ground pepper	sea salt and freshly ground pepper

Mix all together and taste for seasoning.

Cucumber and Mint Sauce

Makes about 450 ml/¾ pint (U.S. 2 cups)

Delicious with a grilled steak and baked
potato, or with lamb, curries or pilafs.
It is also wonderful with fresh salmon and
to my mind far better than mayonnaise or
melted butter, since salmon is such a rich,
oily fish and needs only the lightest and
freshest sauce to accompany it.

Metric/Imperial	American
½ medium cucumber, thinly sliced but not peeled	½ medium cucumber, thinly sliced but not peeled
1½ teaspoons salt	1½ teaspoons salt
300 ml/½ pint yogurt	1¼ cups yogurt
2 tablespoons freshly chopped mint	3 tablespoons freshly chopped mint
sea salt and freshly ground pepper	coarse salt and freshly ground pepper

Sprinkle the cucumber with the salt and drain for about an hour in a
colander. Rinse and pat dry with absorbent paper. Combine the
cucumber, yogurt and mint in a bowl, and season to taste.

A teaspoon of crushed coriander seeds can be added to this sauce
for variety.

Horseradish and Walnut Sauce

Makes about 450 ml/¾ pint (U.S. 2 cups)

Excellent with cold beef.

Metric/Imperial
2 tablespoons freshly grated horseradish
grated rind of ½ lemon and 2 teaspoons juice
75 g/3 oz walnuts, chopped
150 ml/¼ pint yogurt
150 ml/¼ pint double cream, whipped
1 teaspoon sugar
sea salt and freshly ground white pepper

American
3 tablespoons freshly grated horseradish
grated rind of ½ lemon and 2 teaspoons juice
¾ cup chopped walnuts
⅔ cup yogurt
⅔ cup heavy cream, whipped
1 teaspoon sugar
coarse salt and freshly ground white pepper

Combine all the ingredients together and chill in a jam jar with a lid. Serve in a sauce boat.

Yogurt Dressing

Makes just over 150 ml/¼ pint (U.S. ⅓ cup)

This is a delicious, easily made and unusual
dressing to serve with salads.

Metric/Imperial	American
150 ml/¼ pint yogurt	⅔ cup yogurt
1 tablespoon tomato ketchup	1 tablespoon tomato ketchup
½ teaspoon paprika pepper	½ teaspoon paprika pepper
2 tablespoons freshly chopped chives	3 tablespoons freshly chopped chives
sea salt and freshly ground pepper	coarse salt and freshly ground pepper
2 teaspoons vinegar	2 teaspoons vinegar

Combine the ingredients, in the order listed, and taste for the exact
effect you want, adjusting to suit. Always taste as you go in cooking.

Recipes for Slimmers

Of course yogurt is the ideal food for weight watchers; nourishing, versatile and satisfying.

Try my friend Nell's salad dressing. She takes it to the office each day for her salad – it doesn't slop about and it tastes refreshingly different. Simply stir $\frac{1}{2}$ teaspoon caraway seeds and $\frac{1}{4}$ teaspoon celery salt into a small carton of yogurt.

A slimming diet can also be a health diet which will improve your skin and hair and increase your vitality and sense of well-being. Use these recipes for easy carefree slimming and don't dwell too much on the subject of food just now; it only makes you hungry. Try to take up some exercise that you really enjoy; yoga, swimming or tennis, or just walking or bicycling. Save money on sweets or biscuits (or whatever your particular food temptation may be) and spend it on a good suntan oil or some other morale booster.
Good luck!

Slimmer's Summer Soup

Serves 2

Metric/Imperial	American
300 ml/$\frac{1}{2}$ pint tomato juice	1$\frac{1}{4}$ cups tomato juice
300 ml/$\frac{1}{2}$ pint yogurt	1$\frac{1}{4}$ cups yogurt
1 egg	1 egg
juice of $\frac{1}{2}$ lemon	juice of $\frac{1}{2}$ lemon
salt and plenty of freshly ground black pepper	salt and plenty of freshly ground black pepper
sprigs of watercress to garnish	sprigs of watercress to garnish

Combine all the ingredients except the watercress in a blender. Pour into bowls and put watercress sprigs into the centre of each.

Approximately 802 kilojoules/191 calories per serving.

Eggs Florentine

Serves 4

Metric/Imperial	American
675 g/1½ lb fresh leaf spinach	1½ lb fresh leaf spinach
½ teaspoon sugar	½ teaspoon sugar
salt and pepper	salt and pepper
15 g/½ oz butter or polyunsaturated margarine	1 tablespoon butter or polyunsaturated margarine
4 eggs	4 eggs
2 tablespoons grated Parmesan cheese	3 tablespoons grated Parmesan cheese
450 ml/¾ pint yogurt	2 cups yogurt

Wash the spinach carefully and cook with the sugar and just a little water. Drain, press well and season to taste. Place in a heated gratin dish, dot with butter and make four hollows. Poach the eggs and lay one in each of the hollowed nests. Meanwhile, mix half the cheese with the yogurt and warm through. Spoon the yogurt over the eggs and spinach and sprinkle the remaining cheese on top. Flash under a hot grill to melt the cheese and serve at once.

Approximately 879 kilojoules/233 calories per serving.

Vegetable and Cheese Casserole

Serves 4

Speedily made and nourishing, this is an
ideal slimmer's meal, and a good
vegetarian dish. Serve with hunks of crusty
bread for the leaner members of the
family.

Metric/Imperial	American
2 tablespoons sunflower oil	3 tablespoons sunflower oil
3 large onions, peeled and sliced	3 large onions, peeled and sliced
1 large green pepper, deseeded	1 large green pepper, deseeded
450 g/1 lb tomatoes, peeled and quartered	1 lb tomatoes, peeled and quartered
$\frac{1}{2}$ teaspoon dried oregano	$\frac{1}{2}$ teaspoon dried oregano
6 tablespoons yogurt	$\frac{1}{2}$ cup yogurt
225 g/8 oz Lancashire cheese (or any crumbly cheese)	$\frac{1}{2}$ lb Lancashire cheese (or any crumbly cheese)
sea salt and freshly ground black pepper	coarse salt and freshly ground black pepper

Heat the oil in a flameproof casserole or heavy saucepan. Add the
onions, cover and cook gently until softened. Chop the green pepper
roughly, add to the pan and cook for a further 5 minutes. Stir in the
tomatoes and oregano and simmer gently, covered, for 30–40
minutes. Add the yogurt and crumbled cheese and warm through,
stirring until the cheese is hot and melting. (It is best if the cheese is
still in little chunks). Season to taste and award yourself this treat.
  Serve in hot soup bowls.

Approximately 1403 kilojoules/334 calories per serving.

Tuna Fish Platter

Serves 2

Metric/Imperial	American
1 crisp lettuce heart	1 crisp head lettuce
1 (198-g/7-oz) can tuna fish, drained	1 (7-oz) can tuna fish, drained
150 ml/$\frac{1}{4}$ pint yogurt	$\frac{2}{3}$ cup yogurt
freshly ground pepper	freshly ground pepper
$\frac{1}{4}$ teaspoon celery salt	$\frac{1}{4}$ teaspoon celery salt
$\frac{1}{2}$ teaspoon ground coriander	$\frac{1}{2}$ teaspoon ground coriander
1 onion, peeled and sliced into rings	1 onion, peeled and sliced into rings
2 tomatoes, peeled and quartered	2 tomatoes, peeled and quartered
50 g/2 oz black olives	$\frac{1}{2}$ cup ripe olives
2 tablespoons French dressing	3 tablespoons French dressing

Arrange the washed lettuce leaves on two plates. Mash the tuna with the yogurt and season with the pepper, celery salt and coriander. Heap a mound of this mixture on to each plate. Scatter onion rings over all and dot with the tomato quarters and olives. Finally trickle a little French dressing over the lettuce surrounding the fish.

Approximately 1298 kilojoules/309 calories per serving.

Slimmer's Cole Slaw

Serves 4

Metric/Imperial	**American**
1 red apple, cored and sliced	1 red apple, cored and sliced
2–3 carrots, scraped and grated	2–3 carrots, scraped and grated
juice of 1 lemon	juice of 1 lemon
225 g/8 oz white cabbage, shredded	3 cups shredded white cabbage
$\frac{1}{2}$ teaspoon caraway seeds	$\frac{1}{2}$ teaspoon caraway seeds
1 teaspoon Dijon mustard	1 teaspoon Dijon mustard
4 sticks celery, chopped	4 stalks celery, chopped
150 ml/$\frac{1}{4}$ pint yogurt	$\frac{2}{3}$ cup yogurt
celery salt and freshly ground pepper	celery salt and freshly ground pepper

Toss the apple and carrots in the lemon juice. Mix lightly together with the remaining ingredients and season to taste.

Approximately 290 kilojoules/69 calories per serving.

Jaffa Cups

Serves 2

Metric/Imperial	**American**
1 orange	1 orange
150 ml/¼ pint yogurt	⅔ cup yogurt
2 teaspoons chopped roasted hazelnuts	2 teaspoons chopped roasted hazelnuts

Halve the orange and remove the flesh with a grapefruit knife. Cut out all the segment membrane and discard. Mix the orange flesh with the yogurt and pile back into the orange shells. Chill and serve sprinkled with chopped hazelnuts.

Approximately 697 kilojoules/166 calories per serving.

Note To make the variation illustrated on the jacket, place the orange segments in individual glass goblets and carefully swirl through the yogurt to give a marbled effect.

Apple Mousse with Almonds

Serves 4

Metric/Imperial	**American**
675 g/1½ lb dessert apples, peeled, cored and sliced	1½ lb dessert apples, peeled, cored and sliced
twist of lemon peel	twist of lemon peel
300 ml/½ pint thick yogurt	1¼ cups thick yogurt
4 drops almond essence	4 dashes almond extract
12 roasted almonds, chopped	12 roasted almonds, chopped
1 red-skinned dessert apple, cored and sliced	1 red-skinned dessert apple, cored and sliced
1 tablespoon lemon juice	1 tablespoon lemon juice

Poach the apple slices in as little water as possible, with the twist of lemon peel. Drain away the juice and cool. Beat in the yogurt and almond essence.

Spoon into glass dishes and serve with the chopped almonds and apple slices tossed in lemon juice on top.

Approximately 739 kilojoules/176 calories per serving.

Slimmer's Meal in a Glass

Serves 1

Metric/Imperial	American
1 portion of fruit in season (a peach, pear, raspberries, apricots etc.)	1 portion of fruit in season (a peach, pear, raspberries, apricots etc.)
6 tablespoons yogurt	$\frac{1}{2}$ cup yogurt
2 teaspoons wheatgerm	2 teaspoons wheatgerm
1 teaspoon runny honey	1 teaspoon runny honey

Prepare the fruit by peeling and chopping as necessary. Combine all the ingredients for a minute or two in a blender, then pour into a glass and sip.

Approximately 798 kilojoules/190 calories.

Slimmer's Cole Slaw (see recipe page 99),
Slimmer's Summer Soup (see recipe page
95), Slimmer's Meal in a Glass (see recipe
above), and Tuna Fish Platter (see recipe
page 98)

Desserts

Yogurt desserts are infinitely varied: delicious ices, sorbets, mousses and fools as well as syllabub and cheesecake. Andrew Gill's Champagne Sorbet is very refreshing and enormous fun to serve. For a crowning effect, as suggested in the recipe, top up the glasses of sorbet at the table with ice cold champagne.

Pour yogurt over chopped fresh fruit and top with a layer of soft brown sugar, caramelise under a hot grill and set aside to become cold and firm. This is a deliciously crunchy fruit brûlée.

Fresh raspberries and any soft fruit combine beautifully with yogurt. Sweeten with a little runny honey if liked; this yogurt Chantilly sauce is good with homemade ice cream, fresh peaches, fresh pears or meringues.

Coeur à la Crème (see recipe page 72),
Gooseberry Sorbet (see recipe page 108),
and Raspberry Flan (see recipe page 112)

Eggnog Sherbet

Serves 2

Metric/Imperial	American
2 tablespoons runny honey	3 tablespoons runny honey
1 egg	1 egg
2 tablespoons whisky	3 tablespoons whisky
300 ml/$\frac{1}{2}$ pint yogurt	1$\frac{1}{4}$ cups yogurt
300 ml/$\frac{1}{2}$ pint crushed ice	1$\frac{1}{4}$ cups crushed ice

Put all the ingredients into a blender or food processor and liquidise until the ice is quite fine. Pour into a freezer container, freeze until mushy and then liquidise again. Freeze until firm. Serve in two sherbet glasses or coupe dishes.

Champagne Sorbet

Serves 6

This is marvellously festive and a
compliment to any guests, although it is
not too complicated or outrageously
extravagant either.

Metric/Imperial	***American***
350 ml/12 fl oz water	*$1\frac{1}{2}$ cups water*
200 g/7 oz sugar	*$\frac{3}{4}$ cup plus 2 tablespoons sugar*
pared rind and juice of $1\frac{1}{2}$ lemons	*pared rind and juice of $1\frac{1}{2}$ lemons*
300 ml/$\frac{1}{2}$ pint double cream, lightly whipped	*$1\frac{1}{4}$ cups heavy cream, lightly whipped*
300 ml/$\frac{1}{2}$ pint yogurt	*$1\frac{1}{4}$ cups yogurt*
175 ml/6 fl oz ($\frac{1}{4}$ bottle) champagne	*$\frac{3}{4}$ cup champagne*
1 egg white	*1 egg white*

Boil the water, sugar and lemon rind in an uncovered pan for 6
minutes. Cool and pour in the lemon juice. Strain into a freezer
container and fold in the cream and yogurt. Freeze until mushy.
Remove from the freezer, beat well and then stir the champagne into
the mushy ice. Freeze again to the mushy stage. Beat thoroughly and
fold in the stiffly whisked egg white. Freeze until firm.

For a really spectacular finish serve this sorbet in chilled tulip
glasses, and top up each with champagne at the table. Accompany
with sponge fingers or tuiles almondes.

Gooseberry or Redcurrant Sorbet

Serves 6

A delicious water ice for a summer party.

Metric/Imperial	American
225 g/8 oz gooseberries or redcurrants (no need to top and tail)	$\frac{1}{2}$ lb gooseberries or red currants (no need to stem and head)
about 100 g/4 oz castor sugar	about $\frac{1}{2}$ cup superfine sugar
300 ml/$\frac{1}{2}$ pint yogurt	$1\frac{1}{4}$ cups yogurt
15 g/$\frac{1}{2}$ oz powdered gelatine	2 envelopes powdered gelatin
1 egg white	1 egg white
mint sprigs to decorate	mint sprigs to decorate

Purée the goooseberries or redcurrants briefly in a blender then rub the fruit through a sieve. Fold in the sugar, sweetening to taste, and stir well. Mix in the yogurt.

Dissolve the gelatine in a little water over a gentle heat. Cool slightly and beat into the fruit and yogurt to combine them thoroughly.

Freeze in a covered freezer container. When the mixture is beginning to set to a mush add the stiffly whisked egg white. Before the sorbet is firm turn sides to centre and mix gently. Freeze until firm. Decorate each portion with a tiny mint sprig to serve.

Blackcurrant Fool

Serves 6

Metric/Imperial	American
225 g/8 oz fresh or frozen blackcurrants (no need to top and tail)	$\frac{1}{2}$ lb fresh or frozen black currants (no need to stem and head)
about 3 tablespoons runny honey	about $\frac{1}{4}$ cup runny honey
300 ml/$\frac{1}{2}$ pint yogurt	$1\frac{1}{4}$ cups yogurt
300 ml/$\frac{1}{2}$ pint double cream, whipped	$1\frac{1}{4}$ cups heavy cream, whipped

Rinse the blackcurrants in a colander and cook in barely enough water to prevent them from sticking. When they are tender, liquidise in a blender, then rub through a sieve. Cool this purée and stir in enough honey to sweeten thoroughly. Swirl the blackcurrant purée together with the yogurt then fold in the whipped cream.

Serve in a pretty glass dish and accompany with a plate of sponge fingers or almond biscuits.

Yogurt Syllabub

Serves 4–6

Metric/Imperial	*American*
150 ml/¼ pint double cream	*⅔ cup heavy cream*
100 g/4 oz castor sugar	*½ cup superfine sugar*
grated rind and juice of 1 lemon	*grated rind and juice of 1 lemon*
4 tablespoons medium dry sherry	*⅓ cup medium dry sherry*
150 ml/¼ pint yogurt	*⅔ cup yogurt*

Measure all the ingredients except the yogurt into a bowl and whisk together for about 3 minutes. Whisk in the yogurt. Spoon into serving glasses and chill overnight. The syllabub gets thicker when left in the refrigerator, so don't be anxious if it does not seem firm enough at first.

Serve the syllabub with sponge fingers or almond biscuits.

Apricot Mousse

Serves 6

Metric/Imperial	**American**
225 g/8 oz dried apricots	$\frac{1}{2}$ lb dried apricots
50 g/2 oz sugar	$\frac{1}{4}$ cup sugar
1 packet lemon or orange jelly	1 package lemon or orange-
300 ml/$\frac{1}{2}$ pint thick yogurt	flavored gelatin
150 ml/$\frac{1}{4}$ pint double cream,	$1\frac{1}{4}$ cups thick yogurt
whipped	$\frac{2}{3}$ cup heavy cream, whipped

Soak the apricots overnight in 600 ml/1 pint (U.S. $2\frac{1}{2}$ cups) water. Cook in a covered pan with the sugar. Drain off the juice and reserve. Liquidise the apricots in a blender and cool.

Dissolve the jelly in the reserved juice, which should measure about 300 ml/$\frac{1}{2}$ pint (U.S. $1\frac{1}{4}$ cups), and cool to setting point. Beat the barely setting jelly into the apricot purée and fold in the yogurt and whipped cream. Chill in a beautiful glass bowl until set.

Raspberry Flan

Serves 6–8

Metric/Imperial	American
1 (25-cm/10-inch) sponge flan case	1 (10-inch) sponge flan shell
juice of 1 orange	juice of 1 orange
15 g/½ oz powdered gelatine	2 envelopes powdered gelatin
450 g/1 lb frozen raspberries, defrosted	1 lb frozen raspberries, defrosted
150 ml/¼ pint double cream, whipped	⅔ cup heavy cream, whipped
175 ml/6 fl oz yogurt	¾ cup yogurt
75 g/3 oz castor sugar	⅓ cup superfine sugar

Decoration
mint leaves
raspberries

Sprinkle the flan case with the orange juice. Dissolve the gelatine in any juice from the raspberries in a saucepan over gentle heat. Cool slightly. Pour the raspberries, gelatine, cream, yogurt and sugar into the blender and mix briefly. Heap into the flan case and leave in the refrigerator to set.

Decorate with fresh mint leaves, if you have them, and whole raspberries.

Orange Cheesecake

Light and luscious.

Metric/Imperial	American
175 g/6 oz digestive biscuits	12 graham crackers
75 g/3 oz butter, melted	$\frac{1}{3}$ cup melted butter
50 g/2 oz castor sugar	$\frac{1}{4}$ cup sugar

Filling	Filling
grated rind and juice of 1 orange	grated rind and juice of 1 orange
225 g/8 oz cottage cheese	1 cup cottage cheese
15 g/$\frac{1}{2}$ oz powdered gelatine	2 envelopes powdered gelatin
300 ml/$\frac{1}{2}$ pint yogurt	$1\frac{1}{4}$ cups yogurt
75 g/3 oz castor sugar	$\frac{1}{3}$ cup superfine sugar
4 egg whites	4 egg whites
150 ml/$\frac{1}{4}$ pint double cream, whipped	$\frac{2}{3}$ cup heavy cream, whipped

Decoration	Decoration
fresh orange segments	fresh orange segments
whipped cream	whipped cream

Crush the biscuits and mix with the melted butter and castor sugar. Line a 23-cm/9-inch flan tin or china dish, to make a shell, and chill in the refrigerator until set.

Mix the orange rind into the cottage cheese. Dissolve the gelatine in the strained orange juice, in a saucepan over a gentle heat. In a blender, combine together the cottage cheese, dissolved gelatine, yogurt and sugar. Whisk the egg whites until they stand in stiff peaks and fold in with the whipped cream. Pile into the biscuit shell and leave in the refrigerator to set.

Decorate the top with orange segments and pipe a scalloped edge of whipped cream. Cut into wedges to serve.

Dan's Favourite

Serves 6

Metric/Imperial	*American*
1·15 litres/2 pints yogurt	5 cups yogurt
75 g/3 oz dark soft brown sugar	$\frac{1}{3}$ cup dark brown sugar
100 g/4 oz sultanas	$\frac{2}{3}$ cup seedless white raisins

Stir all together and leave overnight, or for 24 hours if possible, as the sultanas swell up in this time. Stir again just before serving to lift the sultanas up from the bottom.

Hazelnut Yogurt

Serves 4

Stir the praline into the yogurt just before
serving to keep the crunchiness.

Metric/Imperial	*American*
4 tablespoons granulated sugar	$\frac{1}{3}$ cup sugar
50 g/2 oz roasted hazelnuts, chopped	$\frac{1}{2}$ cup chopped, roasted hazelnuts
900 ml/$1\frac{1}{2}$ pints yogurt	$3\frac{3}{4}$ cups yogurt

Put the sugar into a heavy frying pan over a low heat and leave quite
alone until it is a brown syrup. Stir in the hazelnuts and pour on to an
oiled roasting tin. When it has set break into pieces, then wrap in a
clean tea towel and break it up with a hammer. Alternatively the
pieces can be put into a blender or food processor and coarsely
ground.

Stir into the yogurt and pour into small china pots or glasses.

Pineapple with Black Grapes

Serves 4

Metric/Imperial	American
1 pineapple, peeled and cubed	1 pineapple, peeled and cubed
275 g/10 oz black grapes, halved and pips removed	$2\frac{1}{2}$ cups purple grapes, halved and pips removed
100 g/4 oz castor sugar	$\frac{1}{2}$ cup superfine sugar
3 tablespoons Kirsch	$\frac{1}{4}$ cup Kirsch
300 ml/$\frac{1}{2}$ pint yogurt	$1\frac{1}{4}$ cups yogurt

Combine all the ingredients and pile into a beautiful glass bowl to chill until serving time.

Yogurt Jelly

Serves 4

Metric/Imperial	**American**
1 packet fruit jelly	1 package fruit-flavored gelatin
150 ml/$\frac{1}{4}$ pint hot water	$\frac{2}{3}$ cup hot water
450 ml/$\frac{3}{4}$ pint yogurt	2 cups yogurt

Dissolve the jelly in the hot water. When cool, beat in the yogurt. Fresh fruit can be stirred into this just before it sets. Pour into a rinsed mould or into a pretty glass bowl.

Yollipops

Makes 6

These are healthy, quickly prepared and
inexpensive. What more can you ask?
(Except perhaps a better name!)

Metric/Imperial	**American**
$\frac{1}{2}$ packet jelly (any flavour)	$\frac{1}{2}$ package flavored gelatin
300 ml/$\frac{1}{2}$ pint boiling water	$1\frac{1}{4}$ cups boiling water
300 ml/$\frac{1}{2}$ pint yogurt	$1\frac{1}{4}$ cups yogurt
2 tablespoons runny honey	3 tablespoons runny honey

Dissolve the jelly in the boiling water. Chill until beginning to set. Beat
in the yogurt and honey and combine well.
   Freeze with a stick in lollipop moulds.

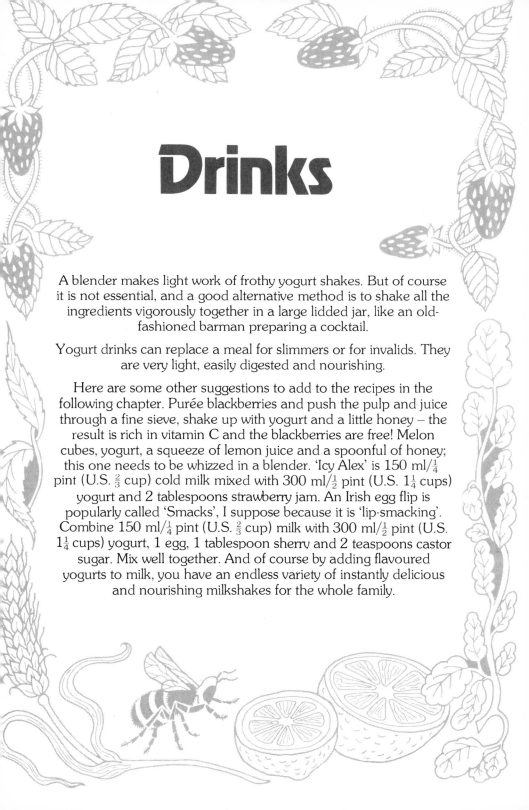

Drinks

A blender makes light work of frothy yogurt shakes. But of course it is not essential, and a good alternative method is to shake all the ingredients vigorously together in a large lidded jar, like an old-fashioned barman preparing a cocktail.

Yogurt drinks can replace a meal for slimmers or for invalids. They are very light, easily digested and nourishing.

Here are some other suggestions to add to the recipes in the following chapter. Purée blackberries and push the pulp and juice through a fine sieve, shake up with yogurt and a little honey – the result is rich in vitamin C and the blackberries are free! Melon cubes, yogurt, a squeeze of lemon juice and a spoonful of honey; this one needs to be whizzed in a blender. 'Icy Alex' is 150 ml/$\frac{1}{4}$ pint (U.S. $\frac{2}{3}$ cup) cold milk mixed with 300 ml/$\frac{1}{2}$ pint (U.S. $1\frac{1}{4}$ cups) yogurt and 2 tablespoons strawberry jam. An Irish egg flip is popularly called 'Smacks', I suppose because it is 'lip-smacking'. Combine 150 ml/$\frac{1}{4}$ pint (U.S. $\frac{2}{3}$ cup) milk with 300 ml/$\frac{1}{2}$ pint (U.S. $1\frac{1}{4}$ cups) yogurt, 1 egg, 1 tablespoon sherry and 2 teaspoons castor sugar. Mix well together. And of course by adding flavoured yogurts to milk, you have an endless variety of instantly delicious and nourishing milkshakes for the whole family.

Coffee Ice Dream

Serves 2

Metric/Imperial	*American*
300 ml/½ pint strong black coffee, cooled	*1¼ cups strong black coffee, cooled*
300 ml/½ pint yogurt	*1¼ cups yogurt*
2 scoops coffee ice cream	*2 servings coffee ice cream*

Mix the coffee and yogurt together, using a blender if you have one. (Sweeten a little if you like, but the contrast with the sweet ice cream is better to my mind.)

Serve with a spoon in tall glasses and float the ice cream on top.

Strawberry Fare

Serves 4

Metric/Imperial	**American**
225 g/8 oz strawberries	$\frac{1}{2}$ lb strawberries
600 ml/1 pint yogurt	$2\frac{1}{2}$ cups yogurt
juice of 1 orange	juice of 1 orange
1 tablespoon runny honey	1 tablespoon runny honey
4 scoops vanilla ice cream	4 servings vanilla ice cream

Hull the strawberries and put them into a blender with the yogurt, orange juice and honey. Whizz until well combined. Serve in tall glasses with a scoop of ice cream in the top of each.

Banana Shake

Serves 2

Metric/Imperial	American
300 ml/$\frac{1}{2}$ pint iced milk	1$\frac{1}{4}$ cups iced milk
150 ml/$\frac{1}{4}$ pint yogurt	$\frac{2}{3}$ cup yogurt
juice of $\frac{1}{2}$ lemon	juice of $\frac{1}{2}$ lemon
1 banana, peeled and sliced	1 banana, peeled and sliced
2 teaspoons runny honey	2 teaspoons runny honey

Put all the ingredients into a blender and whizz until smooth. Serve straightaway.

Orange Apricot Nectar

Serves 4

Metric/Imperial	American
150 ml/$\frac{1}{4}$ pint cooked dried apricots (about 50 g/2 oz uncooked fruit)	$\frac{2}{3}$ cup cooked dried apricots (about $\frac{1}{3}$ cup uncooked fruit)
600 ml/1 pint orange juice	2$\frac{1}{2}$ cups orange juice
300 ml/$\frac{1}{2}$ pint yogurt	1$\frac{1}{4}$ cups yogurt
300 ml/$\frac{1}{2}$ pint cracked ice	1$\frac{1}{4}$ cups cracked ice
sprigs of mint to garnish	sprigs of mint to garnish

The apricots should be soaked overnight, then cooked in their juices and sweetened to taste with sugar or honey. When cool, combine all the ingredients in a blender and liquidise until smooth and foaming. Serve with a little mint sprig in each glass.

Orange and Lemon Flip

Serves 2

Metric/Imperial	American
juice of 1 lemon	juice of 1 lemon
juice of 2 oranges	juice of 2 oranges
1 egg	1 egg
1 tablespoon wheatgerm	1 tablespoon wheatgerm
1 tablespoon runny honey	1 tablespoon runny honey
300 ml/$\frac{1}{2}$ pint yogurt	$1\frac{1}{4}$ cups yogurt

Liquidise thoroughly in a blender until smooth and foaming. Serve immediately.

Grapefruit- Watercress Cocktail

Serves 6

Metric/Imperial	American
600 ml/1 pint grapefruit juice	2½ cups grapefruit juice
300 ml/½ pint watercress leaves	1¼ cups watercress leaves
juice of ½ lemon	juice of ½ lemon
1 tablespoon runny honey	1 tablespoon runny honey
600 ml/1 pint yogurt	2½ cups yogurt
Garnish	**Garnish**
½ lemon, sliced	½ lemon, sliced
sprigs of watercress	sprigs of watercress

Pour the grapefruit juice into the blender goblet. Add the watercress leaves, lemon juice, honey and yogurt, and liquidise at high speed. Transfer to individual glasses and garnish each with a slice of lemon and a sprig of watercress.

Index

Fruit:
  Healthnut special 80
  Slimmer's meal in a glass 102
Fruit loaf, All-Bran 22

Garlic sauce 88
Gooseberry sorbet 108
Goulash 64–5
Grapefruit-watercress cocktail 125
Grapes: pineapple with black
  grapes 116
Gratin of seafood 43
Gulyás 64

Hazelnut yogurt 115
Healthnut special 80
Herrings:
  Norwegian salad 78
Horseradish and walnut sauce 92
Hungarian pork paprika 64

Ices:
  Champagne sorbet 107
  Eggnog sherbet 106
  Gooseberry sorbet 108
  Redcurrant sorbet 108
  Yollipops 118
Icy Alex 119
Irish egg flip 119

Jaffa cups 100
Jelly, yogurt 117

Kebabs, lamb and pepper 50
Kidneys:
Sherried lamb's kidneys 48

Lamb:
  Lamb korma 66
  Moussaka 68
  Sherried lamb's kidneys 48
Leeks:
  Vichyssoise 29
Lemon and orange flip 124
Les crudités 38

Liver:
  Chicken livers with brown rice
  75
  Liver with sage 49
  Louise's yogurt with brown sugar
  21
Mackerel:
  Mackerel with yogurt and chives
  61
  Smoked mackerel pâté 41
Main courses 46–57
Meatballs, Swedish 62
Mint and cucumber sauce 91
Moussaka 68
Mousses:
  Apple mousse with almonds
  101
  Apricot mousse 111
Muesli:
  Apple muesli yogurt 19
  Muesli 18
Mushroom sauce 83
Mustard sauce 87

Nettle soup 30
Norwegian salad 78
Nut and orange sauce 81

Orange:
  Jaffa cups 100
  Orange and lemon flip 124
  Orange and nut sauce 81
  Orange apricot nectar 123
  Orange cheesecake 113

Pancakes, American 20
Pasta:
  Conchiglie salad 77
  Spaghetti with mushrooms 76
Pâté, smoked mackerel 41
Peppers:
  Friendly Hall sweet pepper
  soup 27
  Lamb and pepper kebabs 50
Pineapple with black grapes 116